PRAISE FOR BOOKS BY DON SILVER

Don Silver writes for the Internet on business and personal finance. He is the author of seven books including *The Generation X Money Book* and *Baby Boomer Retirement*.

THE GENERATION X MONEY BOOK

I wish I'd had this book when I was 20 years old. I'd be looking forward to retiring as a multi-millionaire.
—Judy Sterling, Product Manager, AT&T

This is an outstanding book...The author, the aptly named Don Silver, does an excellent job of simplifying information by organizing the book into concise chapters that are between one and four pages long...The book promises tips and it delivers.
—*USAToday.com*

How do you turn $15 into a lifetime nest egg? Use the money to buy *The Generation X Money Book*, then follow author Don Silver's clear, concise and doable advice. This one is well worth a read.
—*BUSINESS START-UPS* (an *ENTREPRENEUR* Magazine publication)

BABY BOOMER RETIREMENT

Astute and provocative.
—*LOS ANGELES TIMES*

more

Don Silver, once again, guides us safely through complicated financial territory with steps that are easily understood and applied toward financial success. This book is the ultimate gift for a baby boomer.
—Cynthia Boman Thompson
    Certified Financial Planner

Read this book and be the master of your own destiny.
—James A. Barry, Jr., CFP
    Host of JIM BARRY's FINANCIAL SUCCESS, PBS

A one-stop resource for busy boomers who want to take control of their financial lives and protect their children, their parents and their financial future.
—*ACCOUNTING TODAY*

The Generation Y Money Book

99 Smart Ways to Handle Money

Don Silver

Library of Congress Cataloging-in-Publication Data

Silver, Don
    The generation Y money book: 99 smart ways to handle money / Don Silver
        p.   cm.
    Includes index.
    ISBN 0-944708-64-1
    1. Finance, Personal.   I. Title: 99 smart ways to handle money   II. Title.
HG 179.S4744 2000
332.024—dc21   99-086728

Cover design by Hespenheide Design (hespenheide@hespenheide.com)

Adams-Hall books are available at special, quantity discounts for bulk purchases for sales promotions, premiums, fund-raising or educational use. For details, contact: Special Sales Director, Adams-Hall Publishing, PO Box 491002, Los Angeles CA 90049, **1/800-888-4452 or www.adams-hall.com.**

First printing 2000
Printed in the United States of America
20 19 18 17 16 15 14 13 12 11 10 9 8 7 6 5 4 3 2 1

Contents

Contents

PART NINE
MONEY-SMART WAYS TO HANDLE PAPERWORK

PART TEN
MONEY-SMART WAYS TO MAKE
YOUR MONEY GROW

Contents

Introduction

There should be a class in school called "Money Smarts 101" to teach how to handle money. That's what this book is designed to do.

Knowledge about money matters provides a sound basis for making decisions about purchases, saving, investing, college and working.

Spend ten minutes a day reading this book and you'll get a quick education to help avoid some of the hard knocks of life.

Better to learn what to do than what you should've done.

What is money?

Although the form of money has changed over time, its main purpose has remained the same—to help people buy and sell products and services.

Probably your first thought about money is that it's only dollar bills and coins. Money is much more than that. It includes checks, credit cards and debit cards, too. To some people money also includes stocks, bonds, real estate and all other forms of investment. And even as you're reading this page, the definition of money is changing. New Internet currencies and cyber forms of money are appearing all the time.

Throughout history, many different objects have been used as money including seashells, cattle, gold and silver.

Paper money first appeared 1,000 years ago in China during the start of the last millennium. Until then, gold and silver were the favorite choices for money throughout much of the world. Marco Polo wrote with some amazement how the Chinese actually accepted pieces of paper as money (it wasn't so amazing since the Chinese emperor threatened death to anyone who refused to accept this paper currency as money).

You'll be dealing with many different forms of money all of your life. You might as well start learning now about smart ways to handle money.

How to use this book

This book is divided into 12 parts and 99 smart ways to handle money. Although I recommend that you start at the beginning and read the book in order, the book is designed to allow you to jump to topics of interest by looking at the table of contents or the index. Every topic in the book will be of interest to you now or in the near future.

PART ONE
Money-Smart Ways
to Think

1. The true value of money

To be smart in handling money, you first need to know money-smart ways to think about money.

Money is part of a two-way street. You trade or exchange money for products or services you want. When you hand over money to make a purchase, it's too easy to forget what you are really giving up.

In other words, you need to remember the value of money. Money is earned through work requiring your time and your life energy. At your age you may have time and energy to spare, so should you care now how you spend them? The short answer and the long answer are both yes. As the years go by, decisions about how you spend your money will affect your schooling, the jobs you take, your relationships with others and the amount of stress and satisfaction in your life.

The problem with spending money too carelessly is that you can become trapped in a job, a career or a relationship that "requires" you to stay there to pay the bills.

Knowing in advance the true cost and value of lifestyle and purchasing decisions can allow you to have financial and personal freedom.

The key for you is to handle (and not too often mishandle) money in ways that are right for you. Understand the value of money and then use your money wisely.

2. The successes and mistakes of others

One of the most overlooked ways to become knowledgeable about money is to find out how money has affected people you know. Ask your parents, their friends and your relatives what they did right with money and what they would've done differently.

Don't "reinvent the wheel" when it comes to money. Use the successes and mistakes of others as a starting point.

You don't need to follow the advice of others. However, learn to be a great interviewer and a smart listener. We all learn best by asking questions, lots of them. And people love to talk about themselves.

Find out how they feel about their material possessions, debts, jobs and relationships.

As you talk to others, chances are you will see how a person's general personality may be similar to a person's pattern of financial actions and inaction.

If you ask the right questions, you'll get a self-taught financial education that's worth years of college.

3. The secret to being successful

All things considered, it's more fun being rich than poor. However, being successful in money matters is not the same as being successful in life. Having a lot of money or possessions may not even make you happy.

Plenty of very wealthy people always seem to want more than they have. If having more isn't always the path to success, consider an alternative. Happiness and success in money matters (and life) largely depend on whether you are grateful for what you do have.

We all want to have nice things and that's healthy. What's unhealthy is when you don't appreciate what you do have and are endlessly wanting what's new, what someone else has or what you can't afford to have. You may never satisfy your wants.

The key is to have balance in your life. Try to attain your personal and financial goals but make sure you're not paying too high a price in the quest, especially when it comes to financial goals.

Think about people who suffer through a disaster such as a hurricane or an earthquake and their home, their possessions and maybe their business are demolished. Are their lives over? No.

Listen to the words of survivors of disasters and you'll hear how "thankful" they are that they and their loved ones survived. It's at moments like these that people appreciate what they do have.

Do you want to be successful? Here's the secret. Do your best, appreciate what you have and you may be richer than anyone you know. Beware of the addiction to always want more.

4. Needs vs. wants—what you need to know

One key way to know more about money is to learn about yourself.

If you can separate your *needs* from your *wants*, you'll be far ahead in the money game and the game of life as well.

Here are a couple of examples.

You may need a car to get to college or to work. You may want a fancier car, however, than you can really afford.

If you satisfy your wants, you may end up working extra hours and days at a job you really don't like. This extra work may mean that you have less time and energy for the other parts of your life.

A more expensive car may mean going into debt that will take years of work to pay off. By choosing a less expensive car, you may gain financial and personal freedom.

As the years go by, you'll have other material wants and purchasing decisions, such as deciding whether to buy a house or a condo. You may want to buy a more impressive home than what you need. The cost to you may be working many extra hours or staying in a job you hate just to pay the mortgage.

Here are four key questions to ask yourself so you can separate your needs from your wants:
1. Am I trying to impress anyone else by this purchase?
2. Am I making the purchase to feel better about myself?
3. How much will this purchase really cost me in time, effort, money and lost opportunities?
4. Am I satisfying a want or a need?

There is no one right answer for everyone. The choice is yours. Just make sure you're aware of the consequences before you satisfy your wants.

5. Time is money

What does managing your time have to do with money? Everything.

If you can't manage your time, you won't be able accomplish what is really important to you. Waste time and you'll have less time for school, your career, your relationships and your friends.

Manage your time wisely by knowing what's important to you. Sit down and make a three-column list with the three most important goals to you right now, five years from now and 10 years from now. Balance your personal, professional and financial goals.

Use this list as your guidepost to make day-to-day decisions about how to "spend" your time.

Once a year take a look to see how you're doing in meeting your goals. If you're really serious about improving your life, review and make a new list every six months.

If you're spending your time wisely, you'll be a richer person by having more time to do what is really important to you.

6. Resisting peer pressure

One of the greatest obstacles to financial and personal happiness is peer pressure. Boy, is it hard to resist.

If everyone else has certain clothes or the latest electronic gizmo, it's natural to want those same things, too.

You know what? You're going to face peer pressure the rest of your life. Now is the time to develop confidence in your own choices and life decisions.

Learn to deal with peer pressure now or you'll be a "sheep" all your life. There's the expression "Just say no." Instead, "Just say me." Ask yourself what's best for me? Don't ask what everyone else is doing.

The price of giving in to peer pressure can be a loss of self-respect and self-esteem plus a mountain of debt.

Why do you think it's called peer "pressure?" It's pressure whether you give into it or you resist it. Be tough. Be strong. Be your own person.

7. The price of being "in" and tulip mania

You've seen many crazes where everyone starts buying the latest fashion or investing in the "in" thing. These crazes didn't start recently. A classic case that infected adults occurred nearly 400 years ago in Holland.

Amsterdam, the capital of Holland, had become a wealthy city in the 1600s. People started to exhibit their wealth by building larger houses. There wasn't much land available so gardens had to be small. The main feature of those gardens was tulips.

Somehow, everyone of every economic class had to have tulips—and not just any tulips, but the best tulips. Tulip bulb auctions started popping up (auctions didn't start on the Net). Many of the buyers at those auctions didn't want the tulips as flowers to enjoy—they wanted bulbs as a way to make money, big money. Bulbs were being resold for large profits and more people became involved as time went on.

You've probably heard of the Stock Market Crash of 1929 that brought on the Great Depression. But the first big market crash was the one in tulips that happened in 1637. Once people woke up and started to wonder why they had traded houses and other valuables for tulip bulbs, the price of tulips went down fast. Soon, many people had bulbs of little value but no money or houses.

Always remember tulip mania before you invest or go for the latest trend.

8. Voluntary simplicity and you

One way to improve your life (and your money situation) is to simplify how you live. The key to living more simply is to really think about (be more conscious of) purchasing and lifestyle decisions. Simplification can stretch your time and your money and reduce stress.

Usually, simplification leads to greater freedom in your life by reducing your dependence upon having "things." You can gain freedom to make college, career and life decisions and changes without being shackled by a financial ball and chain.

Here are six steps to simplify your life:

First, before making any purchase, ask yourself how much of your life energy this purchase will cost. Will you need to work 4 hours, 40 hours or 4,000 hours to pay for this purchase? This isn't a new thought. Over 200 years ago, Adam Smith wrote about the "labor theory of value." Smith felt that the value of any object could be measured by the amount of work for which it could be exchanged.

Second, will this purchase make your life easier, more satisfying or more worthwhile for a period of at least six months? If the answer is no, reconsider the purchase.

Third, do you really need to make this purchase or are you doing it for other reasons such as to impress others (including those whom you may not respect but just envy)?

Fourth, is there a better use you could make of this money such as saving it for a bigger goal, investing it for the future or giving some of it to help others in greater need?

Fifth, do you have room to store or keep what you're purchasing or will you need to rent, find additional space or clear out other items to keep it?

Sixth, how does your purchase affect the environment? What irreplaceable resources in the world will be used up if you make this purchase? Think about all the steps that need to be taken to manufacture, sell and transport your purchase. Your small actions all add up.

9. Frugality

You may define "frugal" as being "cheap." The dictionary defines "frugal" as "reflecting economy in the expenditure of resources."

Our notion of frugality has been shaped very much by Ebenezer Scrooge of Charles Dickens' "A Christmas Carol." Scrooge only allowed his assistant one piece of coal to warm himself while working. Scrooge was cheap. He wasn't frugal.

Frugality doesn't mean being cheap. It means becoming a more conscious shopper and consumer and looking for ways to save money. For example, you can be frugal by buying generic brands (where the quality is no different) or by shopping at sales whenever possible.

10. Short- and long-term goals

Meeting short-term as compared to long-term goals is a constant battle when it comes to money.

Very often, it's a question of satisfying many short-term goals (e.g., to get the latest CDs or DVDs) or putting all or most of them on hold to save up for a more expensive goal (e.g., computer, car, college expenses or a house).

Develop your skills in saving and investing to meet your long-term goals. See the big picture to get the willpower to work towards your long-term goals.

PART TWO
Money-Smart Ways to Live Day-to-Day

11. TV and your life

TV may be costing you more than you think. One of the best ways to find extra time, improve yourself or the world, save money and reduce your "wants" is to stop watching TV. Since that's not likely, read on for two tips that may be an acceptable compromise.

TV is designed to:
- make you want to buy what's advertised
- make you believe your life will change if you buy what's advertised
- convince you that you will be like the actors in TV commercials if you buy what's being advertised
- give you the irresistible urge to buy and consume (that's why we're called consumers)
- most sadly, make you feel incomplete or inadequate if you don't own what's being advertised.

Commercials are hard for everyone to resist. After all, they're designed by professionals whose job is to convince us we can't live without the advertised product or service.

These advertising pros also have the benefit of market research (trying out ideas or approaches on small groups of people before you see the final ad) to see what key words and images will cause us to salivate and be compelled to buy. Add to that the repetition of ads and the day-to-day exposure of seeing our peers who've purchased advertised products and it's hard for anyone to resist TV temptation.

Two ways to beat the advertising pros

Your fingers might outwit the advertising professionals by using the mute button during commercials. Although watching a commercial in silence will still have some impact, you greatly reduce the advertising power of the ad.

Another alternative is just to stop watching commercials by immediately switching to another program (but not another commercial).

Do you want to spend 10 years of your life watching TV?

If you watch an average of three hours of TV a day, seven days a week, you're "spending" over 1,000 hours a year in front of the tube. Instead of watching TV, you could have had a 20-hour-per-week job and paycheck. Over a lifetime of 80 years, that's 10 years of your life spent watching TV.

Am I making up this math? Calculate the numbers yourself. Three hours of TV a day equals 1/8 of a 24-hour day. If you live 80 years, 1/8 of that timespan is 10 years. Reduce TV watching from even three hours to two hours a day and that's over three years of additional free time for you during your lifetime.

No matter how much you enjoy TV, is it worth 10 years of your life? If commercials take up about 15 to 20 minutes of each TV hour, you could be spending three solid years of your life watching commercials.

12. Notebook riches

Do you know where your money is? Do you know how you're spending it?

To get and keep day-to-day control of your money and know where it's going, you need to take two steps.

First, carry around a small notebook for one month and write down every single penny you spend. You'll be amazed at where your money goes and you'll discover easy ways to save extra money each day.

This will help you when you sit down and take the second step of prioritizing (ranking) your spending goals (see Money-Smart Way #13).

13. Getting a handle on day-to-day spending

Do you have enough money to meet all your spending needs?

The way to accomplish that is to prioritize your goals and spend your money by keeping your most important goals in mind.

Having goals in mind helps you with both day-to-day and long-term, larger expenditures. It gives you a way to see whether spending decisions make sense for what's really important to you.

The "right" way for you to spend your money

The right spending decisions are different for everyone. What someone else thinks is a good use of money may not be what you think.

So, you need to create your own plan for spending. With a plan, you can avoid impulsive spending, which is where you spend without thinking about your most important goals.

To get a handle on day-to-day spending, take these five steps:

First, make a list of your short- and long-term life goals. As baseball star Yogi Berra once said, "If you don't know where you're going, you won't know when you get there." Also, writing down your goals makes them more real to you.

Second, track your spending and match it with what you have to spend. Before the start of each month, make a list of the money you expect to receive and what you expect to spend. After the month ends, compare the actual results with what you expected. See where you need to make changes for the next month.

If you don't have enough money to spend on everything you want (or need), where do you cut back? Some expenses are required such as car insurance. Other expenditures such as eating out are optional and can be cut back.

By using the expense notebook in Money-Smart Way #12 and looking at expenses as either required or optional, you'll begin to see your spending habits.

Third, spend (or save) your money first on your most important goals.

Take a sheet of paper and divide it into three columns that you label "#1," "#2" and "#3." Now rank your expenditures in categories of importance from #1 through #3. For example, #1 priorities are your most important goals (e.g., paying car insurance, saving for a computer, a car or for college). #2 priorities are not as critical (e.g., buying extra clothes) and #3 priorities are the least important ones (e.g., buying soft drinks).

Try to meet your #1 priorities to the greatest extent possible before spending on #2 and #3 priorities.

Fourth, become a smart spender (more on this in Money-Smart Way #14 and later in Part Three: Money-Smart Ways to Shop).

Fifth, review your goals every year. At the end of each year, see how well you did in meeting your goals and make a new list for the next year.

14. Ten ways to become an everyday money-smart spender

When you spend, you expend (use up). You may be using up more than money. You're using up the work (time and energy) required to earn the money.

Spending is more than the act of handing over dollar bills, a check or a credit card. It's also handing over a part of you. With this in mind, here are 10 great ways to become an everyday money-smart spender. All of these small items can add up big.

1. When in doubt about a purchase, don't buy it.
2. Every day try to cut down on expenses in some way. Buy a soft drink or coffee every other day rather than every day (besides saving money, you'll improve your health).
3. Reduce your entertainment costs. Instead of spending full price for every movie you see, for half of them go to a matinee, a bargain theatre or see them on video.
4. Eat at home or pack a meal for half the times you'd usually eat out.
5. Shop during sales.
6. Use coupons.
7. Make the library your personal bookstore.
8. Shop with a list in hand and stick to it.
9. Try to repair an item before buying a replacement.
10. Consider buying used rather than new items. The cost savings can be big, especially with cars.

Even small steps can add up to hundreds of thousands of dollars over your lifetime through the power of compound growth (Money-Smart Way #66).

15. The art of asking questions

Whether you're calling customer service about a problem with your computer or a salesperson to get product information, learn to ask questions and to keep asking them until you get the answers you want and understand.

If you don't understand an answer, don't blame yourself. Chances are good the explanation wasn't clear enough. Don't be afraid or embarrassed to ask again saying, "I didn't quite understand. Could you please explain it again another way?"

Then, once you feel it's clear to you, you may want to say, "Let me say it back to you in my words to make sure I got it right."

Be sure to take notes when you ask questions by writing down the item you're calling about, the name of the person you're speaking to, their position, the phone number you called, the date and time you called, your questions and the answers given. Have a notebook or folder where you keep these notes organized.

Then, later on, if you have a problem, you'll be in a better position to back up your understanding of what was said to you.

If it's really important, confirm what a company representative or salesperson says to you by mailing, faxing a letter or sending an e-mail. Think about including a sentence such as "If anything I've written is incorrect, please advise me immediately by phone and in writing." Keep a copy of whatever you write. You may also ask them to write, e-mail or fax you back to confirm what you wrote is correct.

Then if what you see, talked about or purchased isn't what you thought it should be, you'll be better able to document your claims in writing.

16. Cash register smarts

Whether you're making a purchase in a grocery store, video store, department store or an amusement park, pay attention.

Watch the scanner

Mistakes can happen when scanners are used to record purchases. Sometimes an item is scanned twice or a clerk accidentally punches in the incorrect quantity for an item on the register. Other times, the wrong price is programmed into the checkout register.

As your purchases are being scanned in, keep an eye on the amount actually being charged.

Double-check your receipt right away

Before you leave a store, always look at your receipt. Be aware or you may pay (sometimes twice).

17. Some tips on tipping

The word "tips" comes from the first letters of "to insure proper service." In other words, you tip to reward the quality of the service you received.

Since tipping is most often done in a restaurant, here are some guidelines.

First, check the bill to make sure the items and prices are listed correctly. Then, see whether a tip has already been included in the bill (this is more common when there is a group of six or more eating together).

Standard, acceptable service is usually tipped at 15%. There are two schools of thought on whether the 15% should apply to (1) the charges without tax or (2) the charges plus tax. You can decide on what's right for you. The second alternative adds about 1% to the tip.

Sometimes, you'll want to tip extra (a 20% tip instead of 15%) for especially good service. Other times, you'll leave a much smaller tip or no tip at all if the service is very poor.

Remember that tips are not to be paid automatically. You're rewarding the level of service you received.

PART THREE
Money-Smart Ways to Shop

18. Doubling your money while shopping

Saving money while shopping can be a two-for-one deal for you.

Every dollar may be worth two dollars. Here's why. Because of taxes, you (or your parents) may need to earn nearly two dollars for every dollar you spend. So, every dollar you save when you shop can mean two dollars in benefits to you. Every $100 you save this way can be like earning $200.

But keep in mind that you are not making money even when you reduce your shopping expenses. You're spending money and hopefully looking for ways to save when you shop.

19. Get real when you shop

The next time you go shopping, pretend you're living in the Middle Ages and you've gone to a marketplace to trade or barter.

Instead of having brought your crops or your cattle with you,

you've lugged your cash, check or credit card to the marketplace.

How you pay for your purchases will have a big impact on how much you spend.

Buying on plastic makes purchases unreal

When a credit card is used to make a purchase, it doesn't feel like someone opened up your wallet or pocketbook and took money out of it. If it did feel that way, you would tend to spend less (and save more). Why is that?

With a credit card purchase, what feels real is walking out of the store with an armful of goodies. And to think you got all that stuff just for signing your name to a piece of paper that's a credit card slip! The reality of the cost of a credit card purchase only hits you when your credit card statement arrives in the mail.

The unreality of spending with credit cards becomes more apparent when you compare it to spending by cash or a check.

Paying by cash feels real and saves you money

Paying by cash is as real as it gets with spending. It's like trading the cow you brought to market in return for the goods you'll carry home. You'd notice a missing cow and the same thing happens when you pay by cash. As you hand over the bills to the merchant and your wallet or pocketbook becomes skinnier, the transaction becomes real and physical to you and your brain.

That is why people who pay only by cash spend less than people who pay by check or credit card. Paying with cash also helps you avoid debt by allowing you to spend only what you have on hand and in hand.

Naturally, cash can't be used for every purchase (and shouldn't be where you later want proof of payment such as through the use of a cancelled check). But try to use cash as often as possible as a technique to reduce your spending.

Paying by check also helps keep reality in mind

If you write down every check and every deposit in your checkbook register and keep a running total of the balance on hand, you'll stay in touch with financial reality.

If you don't (and hopefully won't) write a check beyond your checking account balance on hand, you have a way to control your spending and make the impact of spending seem more real.

Coming back to reality

When you shop, you need to be aware of what you can afford to spend. Using cash and checks can give you that reality check. Both of these ways make you more aware of what money you really have to spend.

Credit cards remove that reality. What you have with credit cards is an available balance to spend, *not* an available ability to pay.

Make shopping more real and you'll lower your expenses, lessen your stress and have greater flexibility in your life through increased financial independence.

20. Know why you're shopping

If you want to control your shopping, shop with a specific purchase (and purpose) in mind. Shop with a purpose by having a shopping list in hand before you walk out the door.

21. Shop with a budget

When you shop, you need to budget, too. When you budget, you match up the money you have and what you are doing with it.

In general, you have four options for your money:
1. Buy things now
2. Save to buy things another day
3. Save and invest
4. Give to charity

It's a natural instinct to spend money as soon as it's received. For some reason, this usually leads to running out of money too soon.

At some point, you'll need to control your everyday spending so you can save up to make a bigger purchase such as a computer, a car or a house.

Putting aside money for future purchases is part of budgeting. Learn to budget now and you'll have a lifetime tool that will keep you out of money trouble.

Remember the distinction between needs and wants in Money-Smart Way #4. It really comes into play when making a budget.

What is a budget? It's a way of making sure you have enough money on hand for what's really important to you. It's a way to pay for your needs and hopefully, some of your wants, too.

Budgeting your needs and wants

There are four steps to a good budget:

1. Write down your expected income (that might be your allowance as well as your earnings). Start doing budgets for one week at a time and work your way up to doing two-week and then monthly budgets. Eventually, you'll be doing yearly budgets.

2. Then make a list of your expected spending for the budget period you selected in #1 above. Write down your spending in five categories for using your money: what you really need to spend now, how much you'd like to save, what you'd like to spend in the future, what you'd like to give to others and what you'd like to spend on your wants (see Money-Saving Way #4).

3. Make sure #1 (income) is bigger than #2 (spending) or else you'll need to earn some extra money or cut down on your spending.

4. It can be tough to add extra income especially if you're going to school and already putting in a large number of hours at a job. So, the primary budgeting skill you need to develop is how to cut down on short-term spending. If you want to save enough for a major purchase such as a car without going into any or too much debt, you'll need to control spending on short-term wants.

Stay within your budget to find the right balance for using your money.

22. Avoid impulsive spending

The best budget is useless if you do too much impulsive spending. These unplanned purchases are not part of your budget (unless you've planned for a certain amount of "unplanned" spending).

To avoid impulsive spending, you need special protective armor. Since you are continually subjected to advertisements encouraging you to buy more, it's hard to resist impulsive shopping. We live in a society that is constantly pushing us to spend, whether we can afford it or not.

Protect yourself against impulsive spending by budgeting your spending in advance and sticking to your budget.

23. Shopping is not like breathing

Fortunately, you could survive for quite a while if you put your shopping on hold. We are all often unaware of our reasons for shopping and so it helps to become more conscious of why we shop (especially for things we really don't need). Some people use shopping as a way to cheer themselves up or as a form of entertainment.

If you often go shopping (and spending), try instead to develop other forms of social interaction and recreation. Being with friends or family, exercising, enjoying nature, reading a good book from the library or volunteering to help others can be a far more profitable use of your time.

24. Four times not to shop

Thursday, Friday, Saturday and Sunday. Seriously, here are four times you shouldn't be shopping:

1. If you're depressed or feeling low, it's too easy to make unnecessary purchases.

2. If you can get something for free, don't pay for it. A good example is books. Very often, you'll read a book once and never look at it again except to try to find a place to store it. Then, over the years, you'll spend more time and money moving these never-to-be-read-again books with you as you crisscross the country. Think instead about just borrowing a book from the

library. Then, if you feel you really want the book as part of your permanent collection, you can always buy it (and then lug it everywhere you move to).

Borrow but don't buy applies in other areas, too. Sometimes you'll take on a project or need to do a repair that requires a tool you may only use that one time. If someone you know already has the tool, don't spend your time and money to buy it.

3. If you're just trying to impress someone else with a purchase you want to make, save your money and figure out how to improve your self-esteem instead.

4. If you really can't afford to go shopping for an item, don't. Be realistic as to what's affordable and what's really a burden to buy.

25. Eight steps to successful shopping

Here are eight steps to help make your shopping successful.

As you go through the steps, think about how they would apply to the purchase of a computer.

First, do comparison shopping. One of the keys to being a money-smart shopper is to do comparison shopping. Zero in on what you need. Do research on line and through magazines, stores and friends to determine the specifications you need and the product reviews of the various choices.

Comparison shopping falls into two categories: (1) comparing apples to apples and (2) comparing apples to oranges.

Compare apples to apples

If you definitely know the exact item you want to purchase, you can then call different stores or compare prices on the Internet. To make sure you're really comparing the exact same product (e.g., apples to apples), be sure to ask about shipping costs, warranties and return policies, too. What may appear to be less expensive at first may change once you get the whole story.

If possible, personally take a look at what you'll be buying.

Comparing apples and oranges

You may not be sure exactly which product you want to buy. Here's where it gets trickier to do comparison shopping.

Very often, products only list some of their features. It can be difficult to know what's included and excluded on products of a similar type. You can get much of the needed information through the Net or at your local library. Also try calling a toll-free customer service number to ask your questions and see whether there are some specification or "spec" sheets the company can send you that list and compare features on different products.

Then, once you've decided on a particular product, you can then go back to your apples-to-apples comparison shopping.

Second, consider buying pre-owned rather than new products. Just about everyone prefers buying new to old. About the only time this may not apply is when it comes to houses. Sometimes those older homes have a certain charm that you don't find in newer houses.

So why buy pre-owned (a fancy word for used)? Buying used saves money. And in many cases, the quality is the same. You can buy a used CD and the sound will be as clear as a new one. You can buy a refurbished computer and it may be of the same quality and have the same warranty as a new computer. The only difference might be in the price—it's lower.

There are other reasons to consider buying pre-owned products. You may be helping the environment by keeping a product in use that might otherwise go into an overcrowded landfill. Buying used may keep valuable natural resources from being used up to produce, transport and sell a new product.

If it bothers you to buy something used, consider getting the product through a trade or barter with a friend instead. You may have clothes, a CD or a computer that is no longer right for you. Maybe it's the right fit for a friend of yours and they have something you need in return.

Just remember there is a big problem when you buy something new. Right away it becomes "used" anyway. That's the reason you hear a new car loses thousands of dollars of value as soon as it's driven off the lot.

Third, shop at sales.

Some of the best sales are during the off season. For example, once winter ends, winter clothes go down in price. You can be dollars ahead for next year by making next year's purchases during this year's off season sale.

Department stores have certain items that go on sale during a certain month of the year. Call the major stores close to you and ask about their schedule of sales for the upcoming year. It may be worth waiting to make a purchase until the sale month comes up for that product.

One last word about sales. Sometimes special sale prices only apply to certain items and not the ones of interest to you. Don't believe you're at a sale unless the prices really reflect that.

Fourth, save money with newspapers in two main ways. Sales are often advertised in papers. In addition, newspapers are filled with coupons. Some stores honor coupons from competitors' stores. Remember, a coupon doesn't save you money unless you really need the item. But if you do, coupons can be a great way to save.

Fifth, keep ads to show special prices.

Sometimes you go to a store in response to an ad only to find the price of a product is higher than advertised. Usually, this is an oversight on the part of the merchant. One way of getting the special advertised price is to bring the advertisement to the store so any difference in the price will be resolved in your favor. Bringing an ad with you to a store is another way of having a shopping list to control your spending.

Sixth, get value for your purchases. Good shopping means getting your money's worth, not just spending as little as you can.

One of the toughest tasks is learning how to judge quality and value. Usually, quality purchases mean items that will last longer and cost more. With some purchases, it means more durability or strength. With others, it may mean that they won't become outdated as soon.

Quality takes on other aspects in other parts of our lives. For example, in a grocery store, getting good value may depend upon your reading product labels to determine which product is better.

Seventh, learn to negotiate.

Although we don't shop in a bazaar where bartering or price haggling is the usual way to buy, the savvy shopper, knowing there may be plenty of room to negotiate, rarely accepts prices at face value.

Think about it. You'll often see advertisements that say, "We'll match any advertised price." That means that the listed prices in the store may be higher than the competition's and the store doesn't want to lose your business to a competitor. If stores are in essence advertising that their prices will be lower if you ask, speak up.

Don't be afraid to make an offer if you feel a price for a purchase is too high or unaffordable for you. Just say to the merchant, the car rental agency, the hotel or any other seller, "What's the best price you can give me?" or "I can only afford this much." The worst they can say is no. You've got a chance that they'll say yes or settle somewhere in the middle. Why overpay? If you can spot a defect, even a small one, in a product you may also be able to better negotiate a lower price.

Don't overlook the Internet in hunting for bargains. You may decide to make purchases over the Internet or you may use the information you've obtained there to negotiate with your local stores. By being able to show them a printout of how little you can spend on the same item over the Net, you may receive an instant discount to encourage you to make the purchase from them.

Eighth, learn to say no. The most effective negotiating technique is being able to say no and mean it. If you're ready to walk away from a transaction but the other side wants you to stay, you definitely can have the upper hand. This allows you to get a better price or to just pass on the transaction if it really doesn't make sense for you.

26. Shopping smart on the Internet

Here are seven ways to be a money-smart shopper on the Internet:

1. Use more than one *shopping bot* (shopping robot) to search around for price comparisons. (See the Appendix.)

2. Check to see how merchants are rated for service and reliability. (See the Appendix.)

3. Look for Internet coupons and get other money-saving ideas from the Internet. (See the Appendix.)

4. Look into on-line auction sites to find what you need at the right price for you.

5. Look at sources off the Net (such as consumer magazines available at your library) to compare the information you get on the Net. Also, the U.S. government has a free Consumer Information Catalog listing more than 200 free and low-cost federal publications on many subjects. To view/receive the catalog, log on to *www.pueblo.gsa.gov* or call 1/888-878-3256.

6. Have a purpose to your shopping before you start surfing.

7. Be careful in providing a credit card number and other personal information over the Net (or by phone or mail). See Money-Smart Way #38 on Preventing Identity Theft.

27. Warranties

Products (and sometimes services) come with warranties. Warranties are guarantees that usually last for a certain period of time. Some warranties are written out on the box or an insert when you buy a product. Others are part of the general laws of your state or the U.S.

The point is you may have more rights than you think if something goes wrong with a product. If there's a problem, first look at the written warranty that came with the product.

Depending upon how organized you are, you could have a problem finding your warranty information. Keep track of your warranty information by creating one file folder called "Warranties."

In the file, have a summary sheet as the top sheet with columns for:
- item purchased
- date purchased
- place purchased
- length of standard warranty
- length of extra warranty (you may have purchased an extended warranty or you may automatically have one if you used your credit card to make the purchase; check with your credit card company before making a major purchase to see if you'll receive a free extended warranty through the credit card company).

Put the latest purchase paperwork and receipt (or a copy) right below the summary sheet so it's in reverse chronological order with the most recent purchases on top.

Then, the next time something breaks down, just scan down your summary sheet at the top of the file to see if you're still covered by the warranty.

28. How to protect yourself when returning purchases

Before you make a purchase, find out the merchant's return policy. For nondefective items, you may have to pay shipping and handling charges and sometimes also a "restocking fee" of 10-20% to return an item.

Even returning defective products does not always go smoothly. It is usually wise to have muscle in your corner to back you up if something goes wrong with a purchase.

You can get that protection by purchasing with a credit card. If merchandise is not delivered or is defective, your credit card company can assist you in getting the right merchandise, a refund of your money or reversing the charge on your credit card.

By contrast, if you pay by check and the check has cleared a checking account, getting a refund may involve hiring an attorney. That's probably too expensive. And sellers of defective or undelivered merchandise may disappear or go out of business too quickly to allow you to get a refund anyway.

PART FOUR
Money-Smart Ways to Handle Debt and Credit

29. Keeping good credit—what's in it for you?

Just as you use a passport to identify yourself to enter another country, your *credit report* identifies you to lenders and others who want to know more about you.

A credit report shows how well (or poorly) you've been doing in paying your bills, how much debt you've taken on and how long you've had the debt.

If you start out your life paying your bills on time and keep doing so, you'll be better able to qualify for loans to buy a car or purchase a home. Not only will good credit allow you to qualify to get bigger loans to make these purchases, you may get them on better terms (e.g., at a lower interest rate).

Keep your financial house in order from the beginning and your life will go much more smoothly over time.

How you take care of your credit is a reflection of your financial trustworthiness.

If you have trouble paying your bills on time, don't ignore the bills. Instead, call up your creditors (the people/companies you owe) and let them know your situation. They may be able to offer a different payment schedule or interest rate that you can meet to keep your credit record in good shape.

How does someone find out your credit record?

There are credit reporting agencies that provide credit reports about you. Once you've entered the world of being a bill payer or borrower, it's a good idea once a year to look at your credit reports to make sure the information listed there is accurate. If anything is incorrect, advise the reporting agency.

It's also a good idea to get your reports in order a few months before you plan any action or transaction that will involve providing a credit report on you. In some states, you can obtain the reports for free. In others, there's a cost, usually $8 per report.

Here are the three main credit reporting agencies:
- Equifax, 800/997-2493, *www.equifax.com*
- Experian, 888/397-3742, *www.experian.com.*
- Trans Union, 800/888-4213, *www.tuc.com*

30. The best credit card advice

If you take one piece of advice from this book, it's this: avoid credit card debt.

Credit card debt can be a ball and chain following you around, everywhere you go, for years and years.

It's so easy to use the plastic to make a purchase that you'll pay for tomorrow and next week and maybe for years to come. As you'll see in Money-Smart Way #31, the interest rate you're paying on credit card debt may be much higher than you think.

So if you use a credit card, be ready to pay off your balance in full when the statement arrives. If that is not possible, either wait until you've saved enough to make the purchase by cash or check or be sure you can pay off the credit card balance (with interest) within one extra month.

Life went on before credit cards were first used in the 1950s. Now made of plastic, they were originally made of sheets of paper pasted together. Credit cards changed how people shop and spend. With a credit card, people could spend money they didn't have yet but that they expected to have in the future. Having a credit card feels like you own a printing press to print money but it's really a printing press to create bills.

31. What credit card interest really costs

Ben Franklin was only half right when he said, "A penny saved is a penny earned." He didn't have to deal with income tax. I wonder what the Boston Tea Party would have been like today if our Founding Fathers had to fill out today's income tax returns.

These days, you may need to earn up to two dollars to have one dollar left after federal and state income tax and Social Security and Medicare taxes.

The "36% return" on your investment

Interest on personal credit card debt is not tax deductible. Why is that important?

If you are paying 18% interest on unpaid balances, do you need to earn 36% on your investments or earn the equivalent wages to wind up with the money to pay the 18% interest? It will depend on your income tax bracket. The bottom line is no matter what income tax bracket you are in, you are paying off credit card interest with after-tax, nondeductible dollars.

If you have to make a choice between paying off credit card debt or putting money into savings, it's usually better to pay off your credit card debt first.

32. Having the right number of credit cards

This is one case where less is better. To avoid temptation, you should have only one credit card. In some cases, it makes sense to have a second card in case your other card is lost or stolen. That way, you're not stranded without means to pay your way.

Even if you have two cards, use only one of them and pay it off in full every month. If you are going to have an unpaid balance, use the credit card with the lower interest rate.

Credit card use isn't just about dollars and cents. It's about financial freedom. If you get weighed down by credit card debt, you will have tremendous stress in your life and be restricted as to the use of your time and your choices for school, jobs and housing.

There's another reason not to have too many cards, especially unused cards. If you apply for a loan, the lender may reduce your loan by the amount of all of your unused credit cards since you could later access this available credit.

33. Selecting the right credit card

To find the right credit card, you need to do some shopping around. Here are the three key questions to ask:

1. Is there an annual fee whether you use the card or not?
2. What is the interest rate if you can't pay the balance in full each month?
3. If interest is due, how is the balance defined when the interest is calculated? Different cards use different methods and may define the balance differently when calculating interest. (If you pay off your credit card bill in full and on time each month, you will not pay any interest at all.)

If you already have a credit card and are thinking of switching to another one that's offering a lower rate, ask some more questions. The lower rate may only apply for a short period of time. If that's the case, you may end up paying a higher rate down the road.

Also, double check whether the lower rate is only for transfers of existing balances to the new card or for new purchases, too.

34. How to get out of credit card debt

If you're up to your ears in credit card debt, you need a plan of action to dig your way out. Here are five steps you can take:

1. Reduce or eliminate your credit card usage.
2. Call your existing credit card companies and ask them to reduce the current interest rate to the lowest rate they can offer you.
3. Make at least the minimum required payment and pay the most you can on the card with the highest interest rate.
4. Look for ways to cut down on expenses, even a little bit. Use this money to pay down your credit card debt.
5. Consider transferring your credit card balances to another card with a lower interest rate.

If your debt is over your head

If you want to reduce your debt or become better educated about avoiding debt, consider contacting the National Foundation for Consumer Credit (*www.nfcc.org* or 1/800/388-2227). This network of nonprofit organizations offers debt and budget counseling and debt repayment programs. Their services are either at no cost or a low cost.

35. Credit card statement smarts

When you get your monthly credit card statement, review it right away. First, match your receipts against the charges listed on the statement. Then double-check interest charges and any fees on it. There are four ways you may be surprised by your credit card statement:

1. A merchant may have charged you more than you agreed to pay or charged you twice for the same purchase.
2. Charges from someone else's card may have ended up on your statement.
3. Someone may be using your credit card without your permission.
4. The credit card company may have charged you an incorrect interest rate or added charges that shouldn't be on the statement.

If you don't protest incorrect charges in a timely manner (usually it's within 60 days, but you need to read the rules and notices on your credit card), it may be too late to avoid paying the incorrect charges.

36. Smart borrowing: the ABCs of APRs

When it comes to paying less interest on debt for the rest of your life, one term you'll need to know is *APR*.

APR is an abbreviation for annual percentage rate. Since it can be very difficult to compare the real cost of debt if charges are calculated differently, the APR is a way to help compare apples with apples.

When you see a loan rate, you'll usually see two rates such as 8% and 8.107% APR. It's the APR rate that is the more important rate. The purpose of the APR is to measure the true cost of a debt. That way you can see who's offering the lowest interest rate.

But don't stop there. Always find out about any other costs and fees that may be part of the transaction.

And always be sure how long the APR will stay in effect. Find out whether the rate will last six months, one year or until the debt is paid off.

37. Debit cards

Debit cards are an interesting mixture. They look like a credit card but they function like a check.

A debit card is really electronic money. When you use a debit card to make a purchase, the money to pay for the purchase is taken out of your account right then electronically. A debit card can be a good way to control spending since each transaction removes funds from your account.

You may use a debit card for some purchases and checks for

other payments. Here's why. Sometimes merchants or tax authorities require a copy of the front and back of a cancelled check to prove that they received payment from you and they deposited your payment.

38. Preventing identity theft

You need to be careful about protecting your identity. It's getting easier for people to impersonate someone else over the phone, the Internet or through the mail by having essential pieces of information.

In order of priority, the five important parts of your identity to keep as secret as possible are your:
   1. Mother's maiden name
   2. Social Security number
   3. Date of birth
   4. Driver's license number
   5. Address

These pieces of your identity are most often used to prove who you say you are when conducting financial and other important transactions over the phone, through the mail or via the Internet.

When filling out forms or responding to requests for information, avoid giving out all five pieces of information. See if one or two are enough.

PART FIVE
Money-Smart Ways to Give

39. The right time to start giving to others

It is natural to want to have good things for ourselves. In many ways, it's against human nature to take care of strangers before ourselves.

How you look at charities at this time of your life may affect your view of them for a lifetime. You need to answer this question now: "When should I begin giving to charity?"

If your answer is "Once I'm wealthy enough to have leftover money after all of my needs are taken care of," you may never give to charity. Too often as income grows, so do expenses. Unless a conscious effort is made to carve out money for charity, you will never be "wealthy enough" to begin your charitable giving.

Since there are always some people worse off than you are, you can "afford" to start giving to charity long before you are rich. Not only is that the right thing to do, you will be a better person for doing it and feel good about it, too.

And your giving could be the gift of your time, not your money.

Seeing the results of helping another person is one of the greatest rewards you will ever receive. Your time, effort and concern for another human being may be able to change the course of that person's life for the better.

You may also want to consider working on a bigger scale with a cause that will help people in the U.S. or around the world to have better lives.

Start giving now. Whether it's one dollar or one hour a month, make giving a habit.

40. Getting from giving

Volunteering can pay big for you in five main ways:

1. When you help others, you learn more about yourself and what makes you tick and feel good.
2. It doesn't hurt your resume for college, graduate school or getting a job to show your involvement with charities. In fact, the absence of charitable activities can harm your chances with potential employers or others.
3. Through charitable work, you will meet other people, good people who are volunteering like you. They may become your best friends since they share at least some of your values. Personal contacts are also one of the best ways to get ahead in the business world. People get to know you and you get to know them by working with one another

on charitable activities.

4. By volunteering your time, you'll appreciate what you have and be less likely to miss what you don't have. This can help you discover the secret of being successful (see Money-Smart Way #3).

5. Volunteering will give you a broader view of the world and allow you to see how to spend your time and life energy on what really matters to you.

Get smart and start volunteering.

To find out how you can volunteer in your community, see *www.SERVEnet.org* or call 1/800/Volunteer.

Check out Youth Service America and its programs at *www.ysa.org*.

PART SIX
Money-Smart Ideas
to Discuss
With Your Parents

41. Making money agreements with your parents

Money is a very tricky subject. Some parents find it more diffi-cult to talk about money than about any other subject.

There may be many times when you'll need to go to your par-ents for financial assistance (the polite way of saying, "I need some of your money!"). In the earlier years it may be for pur-chasing a CD player or a TV. Later on, you may need help buying a car or paying for college. Eventually, you may turn to your parents to help you start your own business or to buy a home.

In every one of these instances, you'll be making some kind of money agreement with your parents.

It may be a silent agreement where the terms of the agreement are understood (or misunderstood) but left unspoken. It may be a loan or an arrangement where you agree to do something in return that doesn't involve repaying the money. It may call for you to do work around the house or in a family business, to get good grades or to spend time with your parents as the way to repay them.

So how do you make a good money agreement with your parents? As with any agreement or negotiation you'll encounter throughout your life, first put yourself in the other person's shoes. Ask yourself what they'll probably want from you. What would motivate them to help you? You probably can figure it out before asking them for money by thinking about what your parents will want you to do or not to do in return for their help.

Once you figure out whether the motivating factor is you getting good grades, working part-time, starting to save your money or helping around the house, think about how you can fulfill your part of the agreement. Don't promise that you'll work 30 hours a week, save 90% of what you earn and keep up with your studies unless you really can and will do it. Be realistic.

Before you say what you'll do as part of the agreement, first ask your parents what they think is realistic for you to promise in return. Not only will you get a different perspective from them, you will have included them in the decision-making process and in your life. And, you will have shown them that you respect their input and advice. For any parent, that can be a tremendous motivating force to make a money agreement with a son or daughter.

And your parents may even expect less than you were ready to offer. Then you might be able to surprise them and deliver more than you promised.

42. Making allowances for allowances

What is an allowance? No matter what your age, an allowance is your parents sharing their income with you.

Allowances can take different forms. Not everyone receives money from their parents. You have been and may still be receiving food, shelter, clothing and extras while living with them. That's an allowance.

You may be at age where you're living outside the house but receiving assistance by borrowing a car. That's an allowance, too.

Depending upon your parents' financial and personal circumstances, giving you money directly may not be possible or only a limited amount may be available for you.

Some parents tie giving money with something being done in return (e.g., chores) while others give it with no strings attached.

You probably won't receive the same allowance as your friends. Every household is different. Some families have more kids, some have more money, some have special beliefs that go along with giving an allowance and some have special circumstances.

You should feel free to discuss the subject of an allowance with your parents. There's a difference between giving you money and having you earn it as your allowance. You may have one view on the subject and your parents may have another. Although there are rules of thumb on how much an allowance should be, keep in mind that some parents view allowances as gifts while others see them as payment for work or as a reward for putting in effort or achieving results in schoolwork or other areas of your life.

A final thought. Depending upon your age and your parents' circumstances, if you are working you might consider giving them some of your earnings to help them out. What a twist— giving your parents an allowance.

43. Money, work, grades and an incentive to save

While there is much to be said in achieving just for the satisfaction of a job well done rather than to receive a reward, you may feel you deserve a reward or a bonus for good grades or for working. Different parents look at this issue differently. Your parents' outlook will be heavily influenced by their upbringing and life experiences.

Here's an idea: find out if your parents have a 401(k) retirement plan. Your parents may better relate to your request for a bonus to reward good work or good grades if they participate in a type of retirement plan at work known as a 401(k) plan.

With many 401(k) plans, employees are given an incentive to save because employers match all or part of the retirement savings done by the employees (your parents).

If you are working and saving some of your money, you may also want to have a "family 401(k) plan" where your parents act like an "employer" in matching some of your savings. For example, your parents might agree that for every $100 saved by you, they'll add 20% or $20. Then, if you saved $1,000, you'd have an extra $200 from your parents.

A similar approach could be used for rewarding good grades with different levels of rewards depending upon the results achieved.

44. Convincing parents you're different than your sibling(s)

You've been dealing with your parents and their money all your life. What started out as spending money, an allowance or gifts may have taken on a different role as the years have gone by. Now you may be working in a family business or possibly contributing to household expenses through a job of your own.

You may be seeking more financial independence or responsibility (e.g., having a credit card or access to one for which your parents are responsible). The question is whether you are ready for this next step and whether your parents are, too.

If you have siblings who have not approached their financial responsibilities in the best manner, you face the obstacle of convincing your parents that you're different than your siblings. The best way to prove yourself to them is by living responsibly.

Show your parents you regularly save some of your allowance or earnings. Do comparison shopping when you make purchases to show you try to save money where possible. Act responsibly with your money.

Once you establish your reliability, your parents will be more open to giving you greater access to financial responsibility.

Actions speak louder than words. Don't just tell your parents that you are different than your sibling(s). Show them.

PART SEVEN
Money-Smart Ways to Prepare for College

45. How much does it pay to go to college?

Currently, there are two financial benefits of having a four-year college degree.

First, the average yearly income for students graduating from college with a bachelor's degree is more than 50% higher compared with those graduating from high school.

Second, having a college degree gives you a greater choice of jobs for a lifetime.

Of course, not everyone needs a college degree to be successful in life or successful financially. But a degree does help put the odds in your favor.

However, in the Internet economy, it is not uncommon for persons with advanced computer/Internet related skills to be financially successful without a college degree.

So how much does it pay to go to college? College is more than a way to potentially increase your earning power. It's a way of developing interests, interpersonal skills and relationships that may benefit you the rest of your life. You'll be working full-time soon enough. Don't overlook the pleasures and advantages of enjoying a college life first.

46. How to select the right college

Once you decide you want to go to college, you face thousands of choices. Here are six steps to help find the right college for you.

First, determine your field of interest. Ideally, when you enter high school start thinking about what kind of work you'll want to be doing once you complete college. Don't let the task overwhelm you since you will probably have many different kinds of jobs in several different fields over your work lifetime. However, you have to start somewhere.

If you have many different areas of interest, take a sheet of paper and label one half "pros" and the other "cons." Then, write down your top three areas of interest and list the pros and cons below them.

Among the factors to consider for each subject area are: (1) your interest/passion in the subject area, (2) how it will benefit society, (3) the likelihood of your being able to graduate in that field and find a job to your liking and (4) the amount of money and security a job in that field offers.

Here's a word about job security. The work world is constantly undergoing tremendous change. Companies merge and come together, others reduce their workforce periodically to save money and some go bankrupt as they are unable to meet business challenges.

Your best job security is to always be learning and expanding your knowledge and skills.

One way to determine your field of interest is to see it in action and talk to the people working in the field. For example, if you want to be software programmer, call up software companies and make appointments to talk to or visit in person with programmers. Speak to people who have been working in the field two years, five years and ten years. See what their perspective is on the work, their enjoyment of it and whether they'd recommend you enter the field in view of your interests and abilities and their experiences.

Every six months during the high school years (and yearly throughout your work career), repeat this process of listing your career choices, writing down the pros and cons and conducting your real-world interviews.

Second, get college counseling. Just as you should start to determine your field of interest as soon as you enter high school, at the same time you should start thinking about the type of college you'd like to attend. If you're already out of high school and haven't started or completed college, then the right time for counseling is now.

Start by talking with a college counselor. Review your list of fields of interest and the input you've received from talking to people working in these jobs. Then take the counselor's information and gather additional information of your own through the Internet and your local library.

Third, make your list of colleges with the assistance of a college counselor.

Here's what to look for:
- the reputation of the college especially in your main field of interest
- the reputation of the college in general
- whether it's a small, medium or large college
- how close the college is to your home

Don't use cost as a factor yet. There may be extra financial aid available from more expensive colleges so the cost may not end up being higher (or much higher) than others you are considering.

Fourth, find out the costs of your top college choices and how to pay them. Now is the time to look at the money issues.

Discuss with a counselor and check on the Net for the cost of tuition and room and board at each of your possible choices and ways to pay for college, including scholarships and loans. Don't forget to consider travel expenses, too, for visits back home.

Fifth, keep the long-term picture in mind. You may be looking ahead to graduate school, too. Certain undergraduate colleges can help you get into a graduate program in your particular field of interest.

Sixth, look at the big picture of life. The process of applying to college can be very stressful. Unfortunately, part of that process is not being accepted everywhere we'd like to be admitted.

Remember this as you go through the application process. Getting into college or only the "right" college should not be your all-consuming goal. It is not a measure of your self-worth. You need to be a good person in life more than you need to be a good college graduate.

47. Community colleges

The right college for you may first be a community college (also known as a junior college).

Even with the financial aid available at four-year colleges and universities, it may be impossible to match the much lower tuition cost at local colleges.

Generally, community colleges are smaller campuses located closer to your parents' home. You may be able to live at home to further reduce the cost of college. And you may need or want to stay nearby to help work in a family business.

Be realistic about yourself. Not everyone is ready to live apart from parents across the country at age 18 or to deal with the pressures of a major university or college.

And many community colleges offer a quality education that can lead to a four-year college or university. Often it's easier to transfer into a four-year school as a junior than to be accepted at the beginning as a freshman.

48. Calculating a college-size nest egg

The nest egg for a private university will probably need to be twice as large as one for a public university.

For a student entering college in 2000, the four-year total cost (tuition, books, room and board and other expenses) is around $53,000 for a public university and around $106,000 for a private university. As each year goes by, inflation (see Money-Saving Way #69) for college costs could increase at about 5% per year. That means someone entering college in the year 2010 could face public university costs of nearly $87,000 and private university costs close to $173,000. These staggering costs point up the need to start saving now.

The good news

There are two pieces of good news. First, you can cut in half the amount you need to have if you go to a public university. Second, hardly anyone saves up all the costs of college.

Should your parents and/or you plan to save all of the costs?

It is usually unrealistic to assume 100% of college costs will be saved. Whatever can be saved will be a big help. If one-half of the needed amount can be saved, that's a major accomplishment. Generally the difference between savings and costs can be paid through loans, scholarships or other financial aid, including work-study programs.

The effect of inflation on college costs

The table below shows the year of entering college and how 5% per year inflation will drive up private and public college education costs.

Year entering college	Total 4-year cost in dollars at **private university**	Total 4-year cost in dollars at **public university**
2000	106,312	53,156
2001	111,627	55,814
2002	117,209	58,604
2003	123,069	61,535
2004	129,223	64,611
2005	135,684	67,842
2006	142,468	71,234
2007	149,591	74,796
2008	157,072	78,536
2009	164,925	82,463
2010	173,171	86,586

49. Right and wrong ways to save for college costs

How you or your parents save for your college education could cost you the benefits of financial aid. With college costs so high, your parents need to know whether putting money away in their names or yours is the right way to save.

Advantages of saving under your parents' names

It is usually better for your parents to save in their names, not yours. The reason for this is that colleges, in deciding on giving out financial aid, first look at how much money a student has. So, if your parents save in their names and not yours, you are more likely to qualify for aid (or at least some aid) than if accounts are in your name.

Disadvantages of saving under your parents' names

However, if your parents save in their names, it exposes the college funds to certain risks.

The funds could be spent for other purposes (e.g., a car or a vacation).

The funds could be lost due to a divorce or a death if you are part of a blended family (i.e., children of a prior marriage). Especially if this is a second marriage for a parent of yours, your college education fund could end up being divided or inherited by your step-parent. It may be wise for your parent(s) who have remarried to have a written agreement to protect your education nest egg.

Estate (death) tax could be due on the funds.

Your parents' creditors (people your parents owe money to) could get their hands on the funds.

Saving in your name

An alternative is to save funds in your name. Usually this is done under accounts opened up under the Uniform Transfers to Minors Act ("UTMA") or the Uniform Gifts to Minors Act ("UGMA").

In general, with UTMA or UGMA accounts, your parents or the people they appoint retain control of the money as the manager of the account (as the custodian) until you reach a designated age (usually age 18 or 21).

The main risk of using an UTMA or UGMA account from your parents' point of view is that once you reach the designated age, you can decide how to use the savings without anyone's approval. You might decide not to attend college and use the funds for another purpose. For that reason and the fact that having accounts in your name will hurt your chances of getting financial aid, many parents do not set up these accounts.

50. Seven ways to reduce college costs

Here are seven ways to reduce college costs:
> 1. Take advance placement classes in high school that qualify for college credits.

2. Take courses at a community college while you're in high school (during the summer) to get a head start on college credits. These first two steps can reduce how long you need to pay for a college education, give you a college experience in advance and just let you reduce your college workload because you're a step ahead of the crowd.

3. Use military service education benefits.

4. Take advantage of nonmilitary service programs such as AmeriCorps to obtain college assistance.

5. Get all available scholarships (see the Appendix for more information). Because you don't have to repay scholarships (as compared to loans), this is the ideal source of funding.

6. Have you or your parents shop around for the best deal on loans. Loans vary in size, the interest rate, the repayment period and how the family income and assets affect the amount available. Don't assume that if your parents have a high income, you will be disqualified for scholarships or loans. Some are available regardless of the level of financial need.

7. Make sure your family is aware of available tax benefits connected with funding a college education (see Money-Saving Way #51).

51. Tax-saving ideas and paying for college

The federal government offers many tax benefits to help pay for your college education. Although most of these benefits apply to your parents, some apply to your grandparents and to you.

Here are five tax-saving strategies that can help pay for your college education:

1. Qualified State Tuition Programs
Most states offer savings programs known as "Qualified State Tuition Programs" (QSTPs). The plans differ from state to state so the fine print needs to be read.

There is no federal income tax on plan earnings until you enter college and use the plan funds. Then the distributions are taxed at your income tax rate (which will probably be at a much lower rate than your parents'). The earnings may be free of any state income tax.

The plans come in two main varieties. The first type guarantees that money paid in now will pay tuition in full when the time comes for you to enter a college in that state. Another type doesn't guarantee full tuition coverage but you may use the money at any U.S. college.

2. Gifts
Relatives, especially grandparents, may want to make gifts to pay for your educational costs. There are two main ways your relatives can make gifts to or for you.

First, they can give an unlimited amount directly to the educational institution to pay for tuition without any federal gift tax being due.

Second, they can each give you up to $10,000 per calendar year without any federal gift tax being due.

However, because gifts made directly to you can reduce your chances of receiving college financial aid or possibly be spent by you for noncollege purposes, many relatives are reluctant to make direct gifts.

3. U.S. Savings Bonds

U.S. Savings Series EE bonds (issued after 1989 in a parent's name and used to pay for your college education) can be a tax-free source to pay for education. The interest on the bonds is not taxable for federal income tax purposes depending upon your parents' income in the year the bonds are cashed in.

4. Education IRA

Your parents or grandparents may be allowed to set up an Education IRA ("individual retirement account") for you. If they are eligible (there are income limits), they can make contributions of up to $500 each year through your eighteenth birthday. Everyone's contributions together cannot exceed the $500 yearly total.

The earnings in an Education IRA grow income tax free. Withdrawals are not subject to federal income tax or penalties when used for certain college-related purposes (state law may be different).

Since an Education IRA account must be in your name, it could hurt your chances of qualifying for financial aid (see Money-Saving Way #49).

5. Hope and Lifetime Learning Tax Credits for Education
The cost of your college education may be reduced by taking advantage of special tax breaks known as the Hope and Lifetime Learning Tax Credits.

52. Repaying college debt

Just about every college student needs to take out student loans to pay for college. When you graduate from school, you'll probably have both a diploma and an IOU in hand.

Once you graduate, you'll want to be diligent in repaying your college loans. This may be your first important step in establishing your credit history and reliability (your *credit rating*) and you can benefit from repaying your loans on time. (See also Money-Saving Way #29.)

With some loan programs, the lender may reduce future interest charges if you make the initial payments (e.g., the first four years of payment) on time. You may also receive a lower interest rate from the beginning if loan payments are automatically made from your checking or savings account.

Your credit rating can also affect your ability in the future to obtain car and home loans or to get them at a lower interest rate. The better you are at repaying your loans, the better your credit rating will be.

With the most common student loan, the Stafford loan, there are several different repayment options available.

The standard 10-year payback has equal-sized payments from day one.

Or you may choose to start out making lower payments and increase the amount of your loan payments over the 10-year period as you expect your income to increase.

Another possibility in some cases is to stretch the repayment period from 10 years to 30 years. This reduces the amount of monthly payments but it increases the ultimate amount of interest payable by you since you are paying on the loan for a longer period of time.

Sources of information

Visit *www.salliemae.com, www.usagroup.com* or call the Federal Student Aid Center (800/4-FED-AID) for additional information and to use calculators to see how different repayment options will work for you.

PART EIGHT
Money-Smart Ways to Deal with Financial Institutions

53. Checking accounts

A checking account is an account with a bank or other financial institution that is used to pay for your purchases or other bills. That's its purpose. If you just want to save your money, don't use a checking account for that purpose. Instead, use a savings account or other investment to help your savings grow. (To keep it simpler, Part Eight will use the term "banks" to represent the more cumbersome phrase "banks and other financial institutions.")

Opening a checking account

When you open a checking account, the first step is for you to put some money in the account as the initial deposit. The bank then has checks prepared that show your name and address (and possibly your phone number—you may want to get checks without your phone number to give you more privacy).

Over time you will put additional money into the account by making deposits.

Then as you write checks to pay for your purchases or other bills, those amounts will be deducted from your account. There may also be regular fees and special fees deducted by the bank for having a checking account (see Money-Saving Way #54 for more information).

Managing a checking account develops skills you will use throughout your life including:
- learning how to pay bills on time
- determining which purchases you can afford to make now or in the future
- keeping track of your money in the checking account (also known as balancing your checkbook—see Money-Saving Way #55 for tips on this).

If you don't have the money in your account to pay for a check you've written, there can be many problems. The least of your problems will be that the bank will charge you a fee for the returned ("bounced") check (also known as a "rubber check" since it bounces right back to you without payment going through). The merchant you tried to pay may charge you a fee, too.

Bounced checks can also affect your credit rating, too (see Money-Saving Way #29). There can also be more serious problems caused by bounced checks including claims that you were trying to defraud a merchant.

54. How to select a checking account

Checking accounts are not the same at every bank. Even within a bank, there may be many different types of checking accounts available to you.

To select the right checking account for you, do some comparison shopping. Since this type of shopping has a lot of details, you'll want to make a chart to record these details, which are listed below, and call different banks to write down the answers. Then compare the information to make a decision on where to open an account.

1. What checking account fees are charged? Ask for a list of the fees charged on a checking account. Fees may include:
   a) a monthly fee (even a no-fee account may impose a charge if the balance falls below a certain dollar amount)
   b) a handling fee for processing each check
   c) a fee for using tellers rather than an ATM for deposits and withdrawals
   d) a check-bouncing fee if the amount of your checks is larger than the amount of your funds in the account
   e) a fee for getting cancelled (paid) checks back each month with a monthly statement
   f) a fee for receiving a copy of a check if checks aren't usually sent back each month
   g) check printing fees (sometimes you will be given a certain number of free checks when you open an account)
2. What are the ATM fees?
   Find out what fees are charged when:

a) you use an ATM from your bank

b) you use an ATM from another bank.

You could end up paying two fees: (1) an ATM fee and (2) an access fee if the machine is part of another bank's system. If you want to avoid paying another bank's access fee, open an account at a bank with more locations. (See Money-Saving Way #56 for more information on ATMs.)

3. How much are the online banking fees? You may end up using the Internet to handle your banking transactions. Find out the fees for banking over the Net.

4. Is interest paid on personal checking accounts? Checking accounts often do not pay interest. If interest is paid, a higher interest rate may be paid as your account balance gets larger.

5. Is overdraft protection available? If you qualify for "overdraft protection," banks will honor (pay for) checks you've written above the current balance in your account up to a certain amount. The "over" of overdraft refers to the bank covering (paying) checks that are over the amount then in your account. This can be valuable protection for you since it can help you avoid accidentally writing a bounced check. Find out the cost of using this protection. Don't rely on overdraft protection on a regular basis. Look at it as emergency backup protection.

6. Where are the bank branches/ATMs located? If you will be doing your banking in person (as com-

pared to doing it over the phone, through the mail or over the Internet), find a bank that's convenient for you.

7. Are there special deals now? It never hurts to ask. You may receive a certain number of free checks or a lower or no monthly fee.

55. Balancing your checkbook

Balancing your checkbook will help you know how much money is really in your checking account at all times. Knowing your balance will avoid writing checks that can bounce and affect your credit rating.

What does balancing a checkbook really mean?

When you balance a checkbook, you match up your records with the bank's on your checking account.

Your bank will give you a small booklet, known as a *checkbook register* (or a "checkbook" for short). In your checkbook, write down all of your checks, automatic withdrawals and payments, deposits and bank fees as they occur in chronological (date) order, adding and subtracting as needed. If you do this simple math and record keeping as you go in your checkbook, you will know how much money you have in your account at any time.

Balancing your checkbook is the process of comparing your records as of today to a bank statement that shows how much was in your account at an earlier date (for example, the last day of the prior month). (Note: If you are balancing your statement via online, the bank's record of your balance will be more up to date, although probably still not as current as your own well-organized checkbook.)

Your checkbook balance

If you write down every check, deposit and charge to your account in your checkbook register, you can have an up-to-date total of what's in your account on any given day. That total is known as your *checkbook balance*. It's a good idea to write down that total in pencil since your math may be off.

The bank balance

On the statement sent to you, the bank has its own calculation of your latest balance (called the *bank balance* or other variations such as *The Statement Ending Balance*).

Putting the two in sync is balancing your checkbook

Although your checkbook should show every transaction that affects your account, your bank statement will have a time lag and not include transactions such as checks you've written and recorded but haven't been processed yet by the bank. Look at the "ending date" on your bank statement to see where your bank's information stops on the statement.

You need to compare your checkbook balance dollar amount with the bank balance and bring them in sync to see if you've overlooked pluses or minuses to your account.

As just mentioned, the bank statement sent to you won't list checks that haven't been cashed as of the bank statement's ending date. The bank doesn't know about these checks as of the statement ending date. There may also be deposits you made after the ending date on the bank statement that don't appear on the bank's statement.

The steps to balance your checkbook

Note that you may only need to do the first six steps to get your checkbook in balance. The last two steps are to help you handle any problems that may come up in the balancing process.

Step One:
Get your checkbook balance up to date. Write down any bank fees listed on the statement in coming up with your current balance. Go through your checkbook register with a calculator and write down, in pencil, the current balance in your account.

Step Two:
Locate the transactions that weren't listed on the bank statement.

Put the checks returned with the statement in numerical order with the lowest number first. Go through your checkbook register and put a checkmark next to the amount of each cashed check that you have in hand. Circle the amounts of the checks that haven't been returned to you. The circled amounts are the uncashed *outstanding checks*. The bank statement doesn't show the outstanding checks because they weren't cashed as of the ending date on the bank statement.

Compare the deposits on the statement with the ones in your checkbook register. Put a checkmark in your register for deposits shown on the bank statement. Circle the deposits that are not shown on the statement.

Step Three:
On the back of the bank statement or on a separate piece of paper, write down what the bank shows as the ending balance on the statement.

Step Four:
On that same paper, write down the date and amount of all deposits and other credits (pluses for you) that don't appear on the bank's statement.

Step Five:
Add Step Three plus Step Four to come up with a subtotal.

Step Six:
On that same paper, list all of the checks you've written and other debits (minuses) that don't show up on the statement. Total up all of these items on your calculator and subtract them from the dollar amount in Step Five. (It's useful to have a calculator that gives you a tape printout.)

This dollar amount should match the dollar amount in your checkbook register. If it doesn't, then your checkbook register and bank statement are not in balance.

See whether the bank shows that you have more or less than you think you do. That will help you determine whether you should be expecting to find a deposit you didn't write down or a fee or charge that you've overlooked.

Step Seven:
Now, you need to be a detective to find out why you're out of balance. If you see the dollar difference is $9, there's a good chance you reversed the digits (e.g., writing down $21 as $12) when writing down a check or a deposit.

Look at the checking statement to see if there are bank fees or automatic payments from your account that you haven't written down in your checkbook register.

If you haven't found the difference yet, see if there is still an unpaid outstanding check from an earlier statement that you forgot to list in Step Six.

There are three other items to check. Sometimes a check is not returned to you (so it looks like an outstanding check) but it has been cashed and is listed in numerical order on the bank statement. See if there are checks like this that you've listed as outstanding checks.

Then, if you're still out of balance, take a look at the dollar amounts of each check and deposit on the statement and compare them to what you've written down in your checkbook register.

Finally, double-check all of the fees, charges and automatic payments to make sure they're listed in your checkbook register and use your calculator to check your math.

Step Eight:
Once your checkbook register is in balance with the bank's ending balance, write your checkbook register balance in ink. This will help make this balanced amount stand out.

Right above that total put this notation "Bal OK" (balance OK) and put in the ending date (the month/day/year) of the statement you balanced to (e.g., 1/31/02) next to that. This way, next month, you'll know your checkbook was balanced as of the January 31, 2002 statement.

Now, go one step further. For any outstanding checks, right below "Bal OK 1/31/02" for example, write O.S. (for outstanding checks) and list the check numbers. When you go to balance next month's statement, this can be a quick way of locating outstanding checks from prior months. Sometimes checks don't get cashed for many months and it can be time-consuming to go back through months of your checkbook register to locate the outstanding checks. This short notation provides a quick way for you to look through your checkbook register to locate those older checks that weren't cashed as of the last statement and need to be listed as outstanding checks in Step Six.

56. ATMs

ATMs or automated teller machines grew out of the idea in the 1970s of having a vending machine for money.

ATMs can be very convenient but you need to find out about any charges for using the machine, whether it's an ATM of your bank or another bank.

Beyond the issue of fees, using ATMs requires some safety precautions on your part:

1. ATMs use your PIN (personal identification number) to identify you. Memorize your number. Don't carry the number on you. If you lose a paper with the number, someone might access your account.
2. To help protect your account, take your ATM receipts with you.
3. Keep your ATM transaction private. Ask people to please move back if they are too close to you and can see what you're doing.
4. Don't use just any ATM. At night, only use ATMs that have good lighting and safe conditions.

57. Online banking

Virtually every bank allows you to bank on line. What this means is that via your computer you can pay certain bills electronically, move your money among different accounts and check your balances.

To bank on line, you either need to use the bank's software with your computer or access your account through the Internet. Find out what's free and what costs with online banking.

Banking on line may save you time and money by reducing or eliminating the need for you to write checks (and pay for stamps) to pay bills. However, not all bills can be paid electronically with online banking. In some cases, a merchant or other vendor will not be electronically connected to the bank. In those cases, a check still needs to be written by someone, in this case the bank, to pay a bill.

As a result, you need to allow additional time when bills are paid by check through online banking. How much time to allow depends on how quickly the bank prepares checks and mails them out.

There are some bills that you may need to pay yourself instead of through online banking. If payment coupons need to be sent along with a check, your bank usually won't have those coupons. So, if your bank sends in its check without a coupon, the payment may not be credited correctly and you may be subject to late fees.

58. Savings accounts

Just as checking accounts have their own purpose (paying bills), savings accounts have a different purpose—saving for short- and long-term goals.

Savings accounts grow through your deposits and the interest paid on your account. As time goes by, interest is paid on the prior interest kept in the account as well as the deposits you've made. This is called *compound interest* and it is one of the ways for you to achieve your goals and financial independence.

Here's an example. Suppose you open an account with $1,000

and the bank credits (pays) your account interest at 5% per year.

After one year, you'd have $1,050. After two years, the balance would be $1,102.50. After around 14 years, the balance would have doubled to $2,000 (all of these dollar amounts are before considering any income tax that might be due on the interest).

Shopping for a savings account

Since savings accounts may serve short- and/or long-term goals, you may need more than one type of savings account to meet your needs.

The main question you need to answer before shopping for an account is when and how often you'll need to tap into the savings account. The reason this is important is that one type of account called a *certificate of deposit* or *CD* is paid at a higher rate of interest the longer you leave the money in. A CD may also have a penalty that reduces the size of your account if you withdraw money before the end of the specified period of time.

Since shopping for a savings account involves a lot of details, you'll want to make a chart with the questions below and call different banks to write down their answers. Then compare the information to make a decision on where to open an account.

1. What interest rate is paid, how is it compounded and what is the *annual percentage yield?* You want a higher annual percentage yield. The more often interest is credited to your account (compounded), the larger your account can become by having more interest paid

on your interest. The annual percentage yield tells you how much the interest rate will really be as interest is paid on interest as well as deposits.

2. Is there a penalty for making early withdrawals? How much is it? Some types of accounts charge you a penalty if you withdraw money before the end of a specified period.

3. Is there a charge for withdrawals? Some accounts may not charge you an early withdrawal penalty but there be a limit on how many withdrawals you can make per month without being charged a fee.

4. Where are the bank branches located? Having convenient branches or ATMs may be important unless you plan to bank on line or by mail.

5. Do you have any special deals now? In some cases, there are special offers but you might need to ask to learn about them.

PART NINE
Money-Smart Ways to Handle Paperwork

59. Starting to pay bills and file tax returns

If you don't already have a checking account, ask your parents to let you write out some or all of the checks for the family bills so you'll have this experience. Not only will this prepare you to handle your own bill paying, it will give you an appreciation of how much it costs to keep a roof over your head with everyone comfortable inside.

Ask to see your parents' income tax returns. Find out how the amount of income tax due can be reduced by certain deductions and credits and how to plan ahead to reduce the income tax bite. Keep in mind that not all parents are comfortable showing their income tax returns to their children.

60. A system for paying personal bills

There are two kinds of bills: (1) paid bills and (2) unpaid bills that need to be paid.

Your bill paying record is the best indicator of your credit worthiness. To stay on top of your personal bills (and keep your credit record in good shape), you need a system for paying bills on time. A good system consists of the right tools and the right habits.

The right tools

You need at least two files: (1) a "Paid Bills" file for the current calendar year and (2) an "Unpaid Bills" file.

If you don't have too many bills, it's okay to have just one file for all of your paid bills. Keep the bills organized by calendar year. It's easier to locate bills that way, especially in connection with preparing yearly income tax returns.

Put the latest bill on top. It's easier to file papers that way and they will be in order—reverse chronological (date) order—with the oldest bills at the bottom of the file.

If you pay many different types of bills and need to find a bill quickly, you can set up separate file folders for each type of bill. Once you begin listing (itemizing) expenses for income tax purposes, you may want to have at least two paid bills files: (1) one for tax-deductible items and (2) another file for the rest of your bills.

The key is to set up a file system that works for you and how you'd look to find a bill long after it has been paid.

If you pay every bill by check, you can refer to your checkbook register (which is in chronological order) to see who you paid when.

The only catch with this approach is on credit card purchases. Your checkbook register usually only shows the name of the credit card company, not what you purchased or from whom. That being the case, for credit card charges that you'll want to be able to refer back to easily, include a description of the purchase in your checkbook register, too, when you write the check to the credit card company.

Another reason you may want to refer back to paid bills from time to time is to locate a proof of purchase for a warranty on an item that needs repairing or replacing. Look at Money-Saving Way #27 to see how to set up a warranty file (to keep track of product guarantees) that can be used in connection with a paid bills file.

The right habits

Having the right tools (or file system) is only half the solution. You need the right bill-paying habits, too.

You may have so few bills that you can pay all your bills on the same day (e.g., on the 10th day of the month). If that's the case, you just need to mark your calendar or organizer to pay bills on the 10th.

As time goes on and your life becomes more complicated, you will have bills due on many different dates. If that's the case, then the one Unpaid Bills file may not work for you. You may need a 1-31 sorter that has sections for each day of the month. Then, you would file unpaid bills in the sorter far enough in advance of the payment due date for your check to arrive on time. For this system to work, you need to check the sorter every day. Since paying bills on time is important, you may decide to pay some bills early so that you are paying a batch of them at once and having fewer bill-paying days. Then, you could use your calendar or sorter to note, for example, two or three times a month to pay your bills.

61. Storing your financial paperwork

Just as you should keep track of your bills on a yearly basis, you should store your financial paperwork with the same system.

Depending upon how much paper and how many files you have, you may want to store them in a large, enclosed, heavy-duty folder with a flap and tie known as an expanding wallet.

Always describe the contents on a label affixed to the outside of any folder, wallet or box to help you find any desired information quickly and easily in the future. Besides describing the types of records contained inside (e.g., bank statements, paid bills, etc.), always include the year, too.

If you use file boxes, number the boxes on the outside and prepare a master list itemizing the contents of each box. That will make it easy to find records years down the road.

PART TEN
Money-Smart Ways To
Make Your Money Grow

62. Piggy bank riches

Here's a simple, painless way to sock away some money by taking your change each day and putting it in a piggy bank or even a jar. The following example illustrates the financial power of a piggy bank.

Let's assume that starting at age 23, each evening you put that day's loose change in your piggy bank. If, on the average, you feed piggy 50 cents a day and also throw in an extra dollar bill, at the end of every three months, you'd have around $150 to invest. If you put this money in a potentially tax-free retirement plan (a Roth IRA—see Money-Saving Way #77), you could receive it all later on without paying any income tax.

If your contributions average a 10% yearly return (which is the average growth for stocks since 1926), then at age 65, you'd have over $200,000 from your piggy bank. Nice piggy.

63. The payoff from one decision

Even one-time steps can pay off big. If at age 25 you spent $2,000 less than you planned on a car and invested that $2,000 in a Roth IRA (see Money-Saving Way #77) growing on average 10% per year, you could have around $60,000 in tax-free dollars at age 60.

64. The trick to saving money

The trick to accumulating money is to make the saving process automatic. "Pay yourself first" from your earnings, gifts or other money received by you. Put a portion of that money into savings.

If you don't grab the savings portion right away, it's human nature for you to run out of money before you can save it. The reason is that saving always ends up at the bottom of your list of what to do with your money. All other expenditures either have a more immediate, short-term benefit or may prove to be more urgent. Instead, you need to make the saving process so automatic you don't need to think about it.

So put a good portion of all the money you receive into a savings account or other investment.

65. Doubling your money: the Rule of 72

There's a quick-and-easy way to estimate how long it will take for your money to double in size. You just need to know the Rule of 72. It's a two-step, easy process. Here's how it works.

First, pick the percentage you expect your assets to grow each year. The percentage can be the interest paid to you on a bank account or U.S. Savings Bond or the expected growth in the value of stocks or mutual funds.

Then divide 72 by that yearly percentage. The answer tells you how many years it'll take for your money to double.

Here are two examples. First, if you expect your money to grow at 6% per year, then divide 72 by 6 and the answer is 12. It will take 12 years for your money to double at a 6% per year growth rate.

If instead, you expect a growth rate of 12% per year, then 72 divided by 12 gives an answer of 6 years for your money to double.

Ways to use the Rule of 72

The Rule of 72 can be very useful when you're trying to estimate how much money you'll have in your nest egg in the upcoming years.

Assume you've saved $2,000 and you're age 22. You want to know how long it will take for that $2,000 to double if it increases at 8% per year.

Here's the calculation: 72 divided by 8 equals 9 so it will take 9 years to double. After 9 years, at age 31, you'd have $4,000 (2 times $2,000). If the same 8% growth rate continued, then 9 years later at age 40, you'd have $8,000 (2 times $4,000).

To see the power of compound growth (see Money-Saving Way #66), let's play with this a little longer. Nine years later at age 49, you'd have $16,000. At age 58, you'd have $32,000. At age 64, you'd have $64,000. That's all from a one-time $2,000 investment.

Now see the power of an extra percent or in this case, two percent growth per year. You might not think it makes that big a difference but think again.

If the growth rate were 10% per year instead of 8% per year, then it would take 7.2 years (72 divided by 10) to double your money. Over the same time period as the earlier example, the same $2,000 would grow to $113,000 at a 10% rate (as compared to the $64,000 at an 8% annual rate).

Remember that the Rule of 72 is an estimating tool. As the percentage growth rate goes higher, the answer is less accurate. Here's why. To double your money, you need it to increase by 100%. The Rule of 72 says a 72% return will double your money in one year (72 divided by 72 equals 1). Your biggest problem should be having such a high growth rate that the Rule of 72 doesn't produce an exact answer as to when your money will double. Note that the Rule of 72 does not include the possible impact of income tax (see Money-Saving Way #78).

66. The power of compound growth

You just saw how the Rule of 72 (Money-Saving Way #65) lets you estimate how long it will take for your money to double over time. That doubling doesn't happen by magic.

The power behind the growth is *compound growth* (sometimes called *compound interest*). Banks, insurance companies and money-smart people know how to use compound growth to get results.

Compound growth is the reason why the earlier you start saving for college or your financial independence, the less you'll have to put away each month. With compound growth, once you've worked for your money, your money starts working for you.

Although compound growth is powerful at any age, look at two examples that show the power of long-term compound growth and then read the explanation of why it works.

Scenario One

Starting at age 20, Sally puts $2,000 a year of her salary into a Roth IRA (i.e., a type of retirement account that potentially can be income tax free). At ages 21 and 22, she also adds $2,000 each year from her salary. Then, she stops making any contributions. If those three $2,000 contributions generate a return (or growth rate) of 10% per year, then at age 60 she will have $225,000—that's $225,000 from three $2,000 contributions!

Scenario Two

Joe waited until age 40 to make his first $2,000 contribution and then he made $2,000 contributions religiously every year for the next 19 years with a 10% per year return just like Sally. Joe, however, would have $114,000, almost 50% less, at age 60.

The results with compound growth

How can 20 contributions of $2,000 produce much less than three contributions of $2,000? The answer is compound growth.

Compound growth or compound interest refers to the effect over time of an investment growing in value and the reinvested growth (the growth is left in and is not taken out) also increasing over time. With a savings account, compound interest lets you receive interest on your interest. The longer you've invested, the greater the opportunity for compound interest or growth.

67. Diversification

You've probably heard the expression "don't put all your eggs in one basket." The equivalent expression in money matters is "don't put all your nest eggs in one basket."

For example, if you only buy one stock, say in a movie company, and that company has a string of movies that don't do well, then the value of your entire investment may go down in value, too.

If instead, you invest in other movie companies as well, you are spreading your eggs but possibly not far enough apart. Why? What if the movie industry as a whole starts to have lower profits due to a new technology or economic hard times in general? Then, all of your movie company stocks might not do well. (I'm not picking on movie companies—I'm just using them as an example.)

So, ideally, you want stock investments to be spread among many different types of companies and industries. Then if one part of the economy goes bad, only part of your investments hopefully will suffer.

This spreading of the risk among different investments is called *diversification*. Diversification means more than investing in different types of stocks. It includes making different types of investments (including bonds, savings accounts and other forms of investment).

Another way of looking at diversification is by comparing it to your daily meals. Cereal might be great for breakfast but would you want to only eat cereal for breakfast, lunch and dinner, day after day, month after month and year after year? At some point you'd get sick of cereal just like investors might lose their taste for the one and only stock you invested in if you didn't diversify.

Some people diversify their investments by investing in mutual funds. Mutual funds are where you pool your money with other people and professional money managers invest the money.

Even if you invest in many different mutual funds, you may not be diversifying your money. Several of your mutual funds may be investing in the same companies or same types of companies. Many stock brokerage and financial advice Web sites can analyze the diversification of your investments.

68. What's risky about risk?

You probably know the expression "There's no such thing as a free lunch." What it means is that you don't receive something for nothing.

Along the same lines, you shouldn't expect a bigger profit from one type of investment unless there is more risk to go along with the profit potential.

In fact, that's how the world works. With a riskier investment, investors demand higher profits (or the potential for higher profits).

Find the right risk level for you. You can't avoid all risk so take it on with your eyes wide open. Fortunately, you are young enough to probably bounce back from almost any investment that goes sour. But why go through that experience and trauma!

Here are five guidelines on risk and investments:
1. Every investment has some kind of risk. Determine the risk that goes with each of your investments.
2. If an investment sounds too good to be true, it probably isn't true.
3. If someone promises you a big profit with no or little

risk, they probably aren't telling you the whole story.

4. Consider the source when you receive advice about where to invest or put your money.

5. Be careful lending money to friends or relatives or borrowing money from them. It can ruin relationships if there is a problem in repaying the loan or paying it back on time.

69. What inflation costs you

As time goes by, it costs more to live. What costs $100 today will in time cost $200 (or more). The cost of living increase each year is known as *inflation* or the *inflation rate*. The inflation rate changes every year. Some years it is very high and other years it is low. Over the last 40 years, inflation has averaged about 3.5% per year.

How inflation impacts your future financial security
Your investments have to earn or grow at no less than the inflation rate just for you to stay where you are. If they earn any less, you are worse off.

Here's an example. Suppose it costs $10 to see a movie (in time, it will cost at least $10 to see a movie due to inflation). If you have $100, you can see 10 movies (10 times $10 = $100).

If next year's inflation causes movie prices to go up by 10% (i.e., cost an extra $1), then you need to have 10% more (or $110 total) to still be able to see 10 movies at an $11 per movie cost.

If you still have $100 (and not $110) to spend next year on movies, then you'll be able to see only 9 movies due to inflation (9 times $11 = $99).

To know how your investments are doing, you need to know how much your investments are earning or growing above the inflation rate. If your investments grow by 10% next year and the inflation rate that year is 4%, then your real rate of return (your profit or progress) is the difference or 6% (10% earnings/growth rate less 4% inflation rate). The difference, 6%, is how much better off you are after subtracting any increase in the cost of living (i.e., the inflation rate).

What inflation costs you

Inflation gets expensive. Just as inflation affects what you can buy, inflation can eat up the value of your investments over time. Even what appear to be small amounts of inflation can add up to a big impact on you over time.

Remember the Rule of 72 back in Money-Saving Way #65. You can use that rule to see the impact of inflation upon your financial well-being.

This rule can not only tell how long it will take for your investments to double in value, it can tell you how long it will take for inflation to double your costs.

Just divide 72 by the yearly inflation rate and the answer tells you how long it will take for prices to double.

If inflation is 3% per year, in 24 years (72 divided by 3) what costs $10 today will cost $20 then. If inflation is 5% per year, in just 14.4 years (72 divided by 5) what costs $10 today will cost $20 then.

Here are three inflation lessons to learn:
1. It will cost more to live as time goes on.
2. Always calculate how much better off you are by subtracting out the current year's inflation rate from the growth or earnings of your investments.
3. Make sure your investments grow at a higher rate than inflation to keep from falling behind.

70. Getting the right profit on investments

Over the last 75 years, stocks have averaged a compounded annual return of over 10%. (Remember compound growth from Money-Saving Way #66.) During the same period, long-term interest rates and bonds have averaged about half of that. Both of these rates of return are before taking inflation into account.

Within any given year as well as any 10-year period, each of these types of investments has often suffered tremendous losses as well as enjoyed startling gains. Know that every year will produce different results. Interest rates go up and down all the time. Stock prices change minute by minute.

The value of everything, even money, changes all the time. An American dollar buys a different amount of Japanese yen or

English pounds at any given moment.

Also remember, as discussed in Money-Saving Way #68, that the potential of higher returns means taking on more risk. Recall from Money-Saving Way #69 that you need to match the inflation rate, too, just to stay even.

Finding the right profit for you is a personal matter and it depends on many factors including: (1) how soon you need to turn your investment into cash (i.e., to buy a car, pay college tuition, buy a house or open your own business); (2) how comfortable you are in taking on more risk; and (3) how you diversify your investments.

71. Investing without using real money

One of the best ways to learn about investing is not to invest with real money. Instead, pretend you have a pot of money (say $25,000) and plan out how you'd invest it.

After you have reviewed alternative investment choices, cut up a piece of paper and on each piece write down the dollar amount and each type of investment you'd like to make.

Then, put the papers under your pillow and see how you sleep the next week. If you're a nervous wreck from make-believe investments, just imagine how the real thing will affect you.

This exercise will teach you something about your tolerance for risk (see also Money-Saving Way #68).

72. Stocks, mutual funds and indexes

When you buy a stock, you own part of a company. Depending upon how well or poorly the company is doing, stock in that company can go up or down in value. While one company's stock is going up in value, at the same time stock in other companies could be falling.

Whenever you buy a stock or make an investment, understand why you think it's a good investment.

You may need professional advice to help you make investments. One way you may get professional advice and spread (diversify) your money among many investments at the same time is to invest in a mutual fund. Mutual funds are companies with professional money managers that pool your money with that of other investors to buy stocks, bonds and other assets.

Some mutual funds (index mutual funds) invest in companies that are part of a published index (e.g., S&P 500) that have the index's daily changes listed in newspapers.

73. How to read the stock page

Stocks are pieces of ownership in a company. Stocks are bought and sold in different places known as stock exchanges. The main stock exchanges in the United States are the New York Stock Exchange, the American Stock Exchange and NASDAQ.

You can buy and sell stocks through a stockbroker or in some cases, directly from companies.

Stocks go up and down in value as prospects change for a company and the economy as a whole. Stocks may change in value constantly during any given day. Newspapers in the financial section publish the ending daily changes in stock values.

The stock pages in a newspaper or other financial publication list more than just what happened to a stock's value the prior day. Usually, they try to give you a perspective, a big view, by including:

- the high and low value for a stock during the prior 52 weeks
- how much change in the stock's value has occurred since the most recent January 1 or when the stock first was sold, whichever is the more recent)
- information about the *dividends* (payments to stockholders)
- the *yield* (similar to seeing how much interest you're receiving on a savings account, it deals with dividends)
- the *price-earnings ratio* (this shows how a company's stock price compares to the company's earnings— generally the lower the number, the less risky the investment; however, in the past few years, many investors have almost ignored this ratio, especially with Internet stocks)
- the high and low value of a stock on the prior day
- the amount of change in a stock's value during the prior day

- the volume or number of shares of a particular company that were traded that day

74. How to read the mutual fund page

Mutual fund pages may show similar information as the stock pages.

Sometimes mutual funds are listed alphabetically and other times by the group or category they belong to based on certain criteria.

Performance results are usually shown for several time periods including the amount of change in a fund's value during the prior day and sometimes the results for the most recent quarter of the year, the year-to-date and the last three years.

Other information such as a fund's expenses and charges are sometimes listed, too.

For more information on particular funds, look to newspapers, financial magazines, financial institutions and mutual fund rating services. Much of this information is also available on the Internet. (See the Appendix.)

75. Expenses and taxes

When you make investments, very often there are costs that are charged in making or keeping the investments.

There are two main types of expenses: (1) fees for purchases or sales and (2) other yearly expenses.

Expenses

When you buy a stock through a stockbroker, you are charged a fee. Shop around, including the Internet, to find the lowest fees around. But don't stop there. In some cases, you can also get financial advice from the stock brokerage company. Brokerage firms that give advice might charge extra (or provide it for free). See what you need and pay the right price for you.

Similarly, mutual funds charge fees, too. Some charge fees when you buy into them and others when you take distributions from them. These types of funds are known as *load funds*. There are other funds known as *no-load funds* that do not have this sale/purchase fee.

In addition, there are also annual expenses charged by mutual funds. Compare these annual costs of owning different mutual funds before putting your money into them.

Taxes

Mutual funds buy and sell stocks all the time. Even though you may *reinvest* (keep your money in there and not take any distributions out), you share in any gain each year from a mutual fund equal to your share of the overall fund. This gain is taxable income to you for that year (unless the fund is part of a retirement account that delays or eliminates any income tax on the gain).

Some funds are designed to produce less income to you by purchasing, holding or selling the stocks owned by them with an eye towards reducing any income tax for the investors. These funds are known as "tax efficient" mutual funds.

76. Savings bonds

U.S. Savings Bonds have some special features.

Because the U.S. government is repaying you, you know you will receive the expected amount when a bond matures (comes due).

In some cases, certain Series EE savings bonds may be cashed in with no federal income tax due on the interest on the bonds (see Money-Saving Way #51).

U.S. Savings Bonds have traditionally produced interest at a lower rate than the growth rate of stocks. So you may want to diversify your investments. In other words, bonds can be a part of your investments but you'll probably want to consider stocks and mutual funds, too.

As to how much to put into bonds as compared to stocks and mutual funds, take another look at the discussion of risk (Money-Saving Way #68). Remember, in any given year or any given decade, there can be great results or poor results for any investment.

The biggest risk with bonds is inflation.

If you buy a bond, it's an IOU to repay you at some future date and to pay you interest in the meantime. The interest is usually at a fixed rate (e.g., 6%) that doesn't change over time.

If you are to receive 6% interest while inflation (the cost of living) is at 3%, you are making a real return of 3% (6% interest less 3% inflation). If inflation heats up to 7%, then you are really worse off because the cost of living is going up more than the interest you are receiving.

This possibility of future inflation has led to the introduction of another type of U.S. Savings Bond (known as the "I" bond) that increases the interest rate if inflation goes up. This bond has inflation features built in to help your investment keep up with changes in the cost of living.

77. The ABCs of IRAs

There are two main kinds of IRAs (individual retirement accounts): (1) the *traditional IRA* and (2) the *Roth IRA*. Each year you may be able to put up to $2,000 of your earned income (e.g., wages or salary) in IRAs. So, whether you're working part-time, full-time, at a summer job or have your own business, look into opening up an IRA.

There are advantages and disadvantages to each type of IRA.

Traditional IRA

With a traditional IRA, you generally put money in that has not been subject to income tax. While your money stays in the IRA, no income tax is paid on the growth or earnings. Depending upon your overall tax situation, income tax is due when the money comes out. If tax is due, the federal tax rate ranges from 15% to 39.6% under current law.

This IRA is a type of *tax-deferred investment*—payment of income tax is delayed during the growing years and is due on distributions.

With a traditional IRA, you may qualify to take an income tax deduction for your IRA contributions and save on your income tax.

Roth IRA

With a Roth IRA, you put in money that has already been subject to income tax. Just as with a traditional IRA, no income tax is paid on the earnings or growth while your money stays in the IRA. Unlike the traditional IRA, a Roth IRA may allow you to receive the distributions free of any federal (and maybe state) income tax.

There is no income tax deduction for contributions to a Roth IRA. At your age and income level, the Roth IRA's potential income-tax-free benefits may substantially outweigh taking a deduction for income tax purposes on contributions. You may decide to convert your traditional IRA into a Roth IRA (check out the income tax rules and consequences first).

Both IRAs are long-term investments

Look at both types of IRAs as a place to put money away for the long term. Withdrawals before age 59½ (or where a Roth IRA has been in effect for less than 5 years) may be subject to income tax and penalties. However, there are some special rules that may allow you to receive distributions from your Roth IRA earlier without paying income tax or a penalty.

Since there are many rules on each type of IRA (and the rules may change over time), always get advice before making a contribution or a withdrawal.

78. Income tax basics

Whether it's piggy bank change or other money you've saved or invested, you need to get smart about income tax.

There can be federal income tax, state income tax and even, in some cases, local income tax.

Income tax may eat up a sizeable portion of your money. Read on for ways to eliminate, delay or reduce the income tax bite.

Eliminating income tax

A Roth IRA may allow your contributions, earnings and growth to be distributed to you free of income tax (see Money-Saving Way #77).

Delaying income tax

Some investments, such as a traditional IRA, grow *tax deferred*. That means that income tax is not paid until money is withdrawn.

One benefit of a tax-deferred investment is that you have compound growth on your investment and its earnings (e.g., dividends) and growth (e.g., increases in a stock's price) without any reduction for income taxes during the growing years.

However, when you take money out of a traditional IRA, it is subject to ordinary income tax. As you'll see below, that's the worse of the two main types of income tax.

Ordinary income tax

Ordinary income tax is at the highest rate (currently 15% to 39.6% for federal income tax).

Ordinary income tax applies to income like your wages, interest and dividends. It also applies to withdrawals from traditional IRAs (the tax-deferred IRA).

Long-term capital gains tax

Long-term "capital gains tax" applies to profits when an investment owned by you personally (and not in a taxable IRA or other retirement plan) such as a stock or mutual fund is sold that has been held for a long enough period of time. The long-term capital gains tax (8% to 20%) is lower than the ordinary income tax rate.

79. Owning assets outside of IRAs

You may choose to own assets outside of IRAs so you have access to your investments at any time without having to deal with retirement plan rules on distributions. Depending upon the type of investment and the amount of time you've owned it, any gain on an investment may be subject to income tax at the ordinary income tax rate or the long-term capital gains rate.

If you're investing or saving to buy a car or a house in the not-too-distant future, then you may want to own some or most of your assets outside of IRAs. (Note, however, that there are some special rules on Roth IRAs that may allow you to take income-tax-free distributions of your Roth IRA contributions and also to use Roth IRA distributions up to $10,000 to buy a home.)

If you buy and sell assets outside of an IRA, then any gains may be subject to income tax in the year of sale. By contrast, gains on assets held in IRAs are not subject to income tax in the year of sale. So, IRA investments may grow larger over time than personally owned assets by not being subject to income tax during the years before distributions.

Determine when you'll need the money and then you can find the right way to own investments—inside or outside of an IRA.

80. Other types of investments

There are many other types of investments beyond stocks,

bonds and savings accounts including real estate, businesses, annuities and certain life insurance policies.

For whatever investment you make, understand why you are making the investment and how you can benefit from or lose your investment.

Most investments take time to produce a profit. Although some investments may turn a quick profit for you, always be prepared to stay with your investments for the long haul. One reason is that for certain types of investments, it may not be that easy to sell them and change them into cash (e.g., real estate).

Become knowledgeable about owning real estate since it can both produce an income (if all property-related expenses are met) and grow in value over time. Remember, however, that all investments go in cycles. There are periods of upward trends in value and other periods where values go down.

81. An essential 10-step financial checklist

Review this checklist now and periodically down the financial road:

1. Determine your short-term and long-term financial goals and objectives. For example, how important is it for you to own a car or home now or in the near future as compared to your other goals? Since there is never enough money to satisfy all your needs and desires, you need to know what's most important to you now and in the long run.

2. Start saving as soon as possible.
3. Diversify investments (don't put all of your nest eggs in the same basket).
4. Take the time and effort to keep track of how your investments are doing (even if you have a financial advisor).
5. Consider the effect of inflation.
6. Assess your risk comfort level before you make an investment.
7. Get professional advice before moving your retirement assets when you leave your job. Different approaches can cost or save you hundreds of thousands of dollars.
8. Select your financial advisor very carefully.
9. Consider the effect of income taxes, including state taxes.
10. Look into making the maximum contributions to tax-deferred retirement plans where your employer matches at least part of your contribution (e.g., 401(k) plans—see Money-Saving Way #88).

PART ELEVEN
Money-Smart Ways to Work

82. The best job for you

During your lifetime, you may have seven to 10 different jobs and possibly five careers. So what is the best first (or second or third) job for you?

Sit down and figure out what excites you. Then look for a job that includes your passion or may lead to a job that does. Think ahead so you don't waste years of your life.

The wrong jobs can ruin your health. The right ones can enhance your life and as well as other lives around you.

Making a lot of money can help. But more important is controlling your spending and learning to save so you'll have the *financial independence to do the work you love* even if it does not pay as much as you'd like.

And remember this. You are not your work. What you do for work is part of you as a human being but it is not your entirety. Be the best you can be at whatever you choose to do.

83. Part-time work

Working part-time can be valuable experience in many ways.

Besides the money you earn, every position you take on is a learning experience. Use part-time work experiences to discover what work you'd like to do in the future and what you'll want to avoid. Find out what certain professions or jobs are like before you invest years of schooling in the field.

You can also use this work experience to learn about people and to see how they interact in the workplace, which may be very different from how they act in other situations.

Finally, part-time work can be an important part of your future resume or college/graduate school application showing the responsibilities you've taken on and the breadth of experience you're bringing with you.

84. Get it in writing

When you apply for a job, you usually have many interviews. The topics of discussion include the type of work, your compensation, the benefits and your future with the company.

Finally, you may be offered a job. Usually, it's a verbal offer, not a written one.

There will probably come a time when you choose or are forced to leave the job. At that point, there may be misunderstandings (or worse) about what you were promised when you first accepted the job.

A way to minimize or avoid problems down the employment (or unemployment) road is to get your employer's promises and descriptions in writing before you start the job. If you're told it's unnecessary to put them in writing, think about what might happen if the person making the promises to you becomes disabled, dies, leaves the company or has a bad memory about that pre-employment discussion with you. You may have a difficult time confirming your understanding of the job requirements and benefits.

What you should have in hand before you start a job is:
- a detailed description of your job so there's no confusion about what is expected and the nature of the work you'll be doing
- the days and hours you'll be expected to work
- medical, vacation and retirement benefits
- compensation

The bottom line is to get it in writing *before* you start your job.

85. Checking out the retirement benefits

Before accepting a job, find out the details of the retirement plan at work.

Ask for a *Summary Plan Description* ("SPD") from your employer that tells you how retirement benefits are calculated and paid out. Read the description and ask questions until you really understand it.

There are three things to look for in the SPD:

1. How much you can contribute to your retirement account
2. How much your employer will be contributing
3. How soon or how long it will take for employer contributions and their earnings to belong to you

Your company retirement plan may be more important to you in the long run than Social Security benefits. Take the time to become educated. When you receive your employer's retirement plan statement each year, double-check it.

Before changing jobs and giving up your current retirement plan benefits, look at the new company's SPD to see what's in store for you.

86. A few words about stock options

It is becoming increasingly common to receive stock options from an employer as part of a compensation package upon being hired. These options allow you to purchase shares in the company at a bargain price.

Stock options are sometimes used as a tradeoff for your taking a lower salary. Keep the following in mind as you ponder the value of these options.

First, you usually have to earn these options by working for the company for a period of time. For example, you may earn 25% of the options for each year of work, which means it would take four years for you to own all of your options.

Don't assume owning options is automatically a way to a fortune (although it might be). Options have value if the stock in the company is worth more than the bargain purchase price offered to you. Stocks go up and down in value. What was your bargain price to buy stock may turn out to be not that big a bargain.

Finally, you may lose your job before you've earned all or any part of your options.

87. How to develop the saving habit

Saving is a habit. Once you start saving, you'll be hooked for life.

A one-year savings plan

Once you've got your debt under control (see Part Four), it's time to take the first saving step. Aim low and try to save 1% of your income in the first month. If you earn $2,000 per month, try to save $20 (the piggy bank technique in Money-Saving Way #62 should make this easy to do).

The next month, try to save 2% of your income ($40 in this example). For the next three months, increase your percentage by 1% per month (3% or $60, in the third month, 4% or $80 in the fourth month and 5% or $100 in the fifth month with this $2,000 salary per month example). If you miss your goal one month, try to reach it the next month.

Try to keep up the 5% per month saving schedule for the next seven months to complete the year.

Don't get discouraged if you can't save 5% every month. Remember, if you miss your goal one month, try to reach it the next month.

You may want to save more in a 401(k) retirement plan if your company matches a higher savings level by you (see Money-Saving Way #88).

The year-two savings plan

You can stay at this 5% level for a couple of years or if you're really serious about protecting your future, read on for year two.

If all goes well, then in year two, try to save 1% more each month for the first five months (6% the first month, 7% the second month, 8% the third month, 9% the third month and 10% the fourth month). Then, stay at the 10% level for the next few years unless you can put even more away.

Again, if you can't reach the 10% goal, do the best you can. The idea is to develop the saving habit and maximize your savings while you're young. That way, compound growth will do a lot of the work for you over time to build your golden nest egg.

88. 401(k) plan tips

If you have a retirement plan at work, chances are it's a 401(k) plan. A 401(k) plans delays income tax until the retirement funds are withdrawn (i.e., it's a tax-deferred investment—see Money-Saving Way #78). This allows your nest egg to grow each year without income tax taking a bite during the growing years.

Here are five tips on your 401(k) plan:

First, don't say no to free money. Although you, the employee, put in most of the contributions, usually your employer will match at least some of your contributions (up to certain limits).

If your company has one of those "matching" 401(k) plans and you're not participating at all or not participating to the fullest extent possible, you're giving up free money. Over the long haul, you could be passing up tens or hundreds of thousands of dollars including the growth of employer contributions.

Second, your 401(k) is not an ATM window. You may be able to borrow from your 401(k) for your short-term needs. But this is a retirement fund. If this isn't enough to convince you to resist temptation, remember that when you pay back your 401(k) loan, you're using after-tax money to do so and you may not receive an income tax deduction on the interest you're paying back. Also, if you leave your job and don't repay your loan before "rolling over" the 401(k) directly to a new employer's 401(k) plan or an IRA custodian, you've just received a "distribution" (withdrawal) subject to income tax.

Third, leaving a job and dealing with your 401(k) can be complicated. You may be able to leave the 401(k) money there, cash it in, transfer it a new employer's 401(k) plan or roll it over to an IRA. Check with your company's 401(k) administrator before making a decision.

You may want to leave your retirement account in your former employer's retirement plan. Here's why. If you leave the company, withdraw your retirement account and later return to work for the same (or related) company, you may not receive credit under the retirement plan for your first work period. Take a look at the company's Summary Plan Description (See Money-Saving Way #85) and obtain advice before making any decisions.

If you decide to roll your 401(k) money over to an IRA, don't count on being able to put it back into another 401(k) unless you rolled it into a special IRA known as a "conduit IRA."

Fourth, avoid early withdrawals that incur penalties. Although withdrawals are subject to income tax, there are times you may be able to avoid penalties. If you're not careful, early withdrawals could cause you to owe not only income tax on the withdrawn amount but also penalties.

Fifth, 401(k) investments require your attention. At least once a year, look at how your 401(k) investments are doing and whether they're meeting your long-term goals.

89. Preventing Social InSecurity

Once you start working, you should be concerned about Social Security. When you think of Social Security, you usually just think of retirement benefits. But Social Security may also provide an additional package of benefits to you, a spouse and children long before retirement if you become severely disabled. Survivors' benefits may be paid, too, after your death. All of these benefits could amount to hundreds of thousands of dollars.

To avoid being shortchanged, you need to make sure Social Security has recorded your earnings correctly because it is your earnings that determine the benefit amounts for you and certain family members.

When you or your family members apply for any of these possible Social Security benefits, how will you or they know if the benefits are based on the correct amount of your earnings? There is a simple way to find out and it costs one stamp every three years.

Form SSA-7004

To keep an eye on the information being used by Social Security, you need to complete a *Request for Earnings and Benefit Estimate Statement* (Form SSA-7004) at least every three years.

The form is free and it's easy to obtain—log on to *www.ssa.gov* or call 1/800-772-1213 to order the form. Then just fill out the simple form and mail it to the Social Security Administration. Social Security will mail a listing of your earnings (according to their records) and a projection of your Social Security retirement, disability and survivor benefits. You just need to compare your earnings records with the benefit statement to determine whether the Social Security records are accurate. If there is any mistake in their records, you should have it corrected before it's too late. You have three years, three months and 15 days after the year in which the earnings were earned to report a needed correction.

Here are two examples of mistakes that could have significant consequences. A digit may be left off (changing $31,000 to $3,100) or digits may be reversed (changing $31,000 to $13,000).

The name is the game
Always fill in your payroll forms exactly the same way. Don't sometimes use a full middle name and other times just an initial. Your best bet is to always use the exact name on your Social Security card as on your employment forms, including W-2 forms.

And for women who change their names upon marriage or divorce, make sure you advise Social Security of all name changes.

The time to check your Social Security records is long before benefits are to be claimed. In the year 2060 you probably won't be able to find your tax returns to verify your earnings in the early 2000s. And even if you could locate those records, it would be too late under the law to make Social Security correct its records. The law makes it your responsibility to be sure Social Security lists your earnings correctly. Pay some attention to Social Security now so you don't lose out in the future.

90. Becoming an entrepreneur

It can be a great thrill and accomplishment to own your own business. It can also be one of the scariest and most financially dangerous steps you can take. Eight out of every ten businesses fail.

Not everyone is cut out to be an entrepreneur. Successful entrepreneurs have a special kind of personality that includes self-reliance, an ability to make decisions quickly and a belief in themselves and their business.

Before you plunk down your money (or your relatives' money) or borrow elsewhere to start a business, do yourself a favor and go to your local library to get the book *Fail-Proof Your Business: Beat the Odds and Be Successful* by Paul E. Adams (or call 800/ 888-4452 to order it). Adams is a successful entrepreneur who has had several businesses, including one on the brink of disaster that he brought back to success. When it comes to small businesses, Adams knows what can go wrong (and how to prevent it) and he gives you the inside secrets of business success.

PART TWELVE
Money-Smart Ideas
For the Future

91. An apple a day and health insurance

Take good care of yourself. You may think you're indestructible now but how will you be at age 40 or 50 if you live your life carelessly or even recklessly? Pay attention to diet and exercise and chances are, you'll live a lot longer than that.

Health is more important than money for the quality of your life.

And part of taking care of your health is having health insurance. If you wait until you're sick to apply for insurance, you may not be able to get insurance or your medical condition may not be covered at all (or until a lengthy waiting period goes by).

92. Disability insurance

Disability insurance provides you with an income when you're too disabled to work. Even if you have a disability policy through work, you may want to have one outside of work. Why? If you lose your job, you may lose your disability insurance, too.

Disability policies are not all the same. They can vary widely in cost and benefits. In general, there are two benefits from purchasing a policy while you are younger: (1) the cost is lower and (2) you are still insurable and not subject to a health condition that may disqualify you from coverage.

93. Life insurance

You may not need life insurance for quite a while. You may never need life insurance. When you die, life insurance provides a lump sum payment of money to *beneficiaries* (people you name to receive the money). Certain types of life insurance (e.g., *cash value*) may also have an investment component.

Among the events that may cause a need for a large sum of money from life insurance are buying a house or condo, getting married or having children.

Before you buy life insurance, always ask yourself and your life insurance agent these three questions:
1. Why do I need this insurance?
2. What is the most this policy will cost me and for how many years under a worst-case scenario?
3. How much will I lose if I decide to cancel the policy early?

Buying the right amount and kind of life insurance

Analyze your purpose in buying a policy to determine the right amount and kind of life insurance you need.

The amount of insurance depends upon why you are buying the insurance (e.g., to insure a good standard of living for your loved ones).

There are two main types of life insurance: *cash value* (which includes "whole life insurance") and *term*. There are variations of each type of policy.

Term insurance

Term insurance is the easier one to understand. Term insurance is like renting insurance—as long as you pay your premium, a death benefit will be paid. You don't own anything with term insurance. If you stop paying the premium, you walk away with nothing and no death benefit is payable.

Term insurance is more appropriate for shorter-term needs. Term insurance premium costs are lower at the beginning than cash value life insurance but they may increase rapidly as one gets older (since the risk of dying increases over time, too).

Cash value (and whole life) insurance

Cash value life insurance combines term insurance (it provides a death benefit) with a tax-deferred investment. A common type of cash value life insurance is whole life insurance.

Cash value life insurance is generally intended to be lifelong insurance (rather than for a shorter term) and it costs more than term insurance in the earlier years.

Get a sound company

As with any insurance, make sure the insurance company is rated highly by A.M. Best, Moody's, Standard & Poor's, Weiss Research and Duff & Phelps. Get ratings from your life insurance agent, the Net or your local library. Since life insurance is a long-term investment, you'll need a well-established and financially-sound company when the time comes to collect proceeds.

94. Naming life insurance & retirement plan beneficiaries

Here are two key tips in naming *beneficiaries* (one or more persons who will receive the financial "benefits" upon your death):

1. Keep your beneficiary designations up to date if circumstances change.
2. Name backup ("contingent," "secondary") beneficiaries in case your first choice does not survive you.

95. Buying a home

To buy or not to buy, that is the question.

There are financial and psychological benefits of owning a home.

Buying, rather than renting, can result in owning a substantial asset (especially once the loan has been paid off). When you make mortgage payments, you are doing a form of saving. And the interest portion of mortgage payments is usually deductible from your income tax (reducing your income tax bill). There are also special rules on selling a home that may make most or all of the gain income tax free.

On the other hand, homes can go down in value, even below what you owe on the property. You can lose your entire investment.

In general, if you think you've settled down and you're going to own your home for at least five years, then it's probably a good idea to buy one. However, if your work situation is not stable enough to know that you'll live in the same area, think twice about the selling costs you'll need to pay and what will happen if you can't sell your home when you need to move. Renting, instead of owning, can be a very wise move in many cases.

How reliable you've been in paying your other bills can affect your home loan (mortgage). If you're considered a good credit risk, you'll have a much easier time qualifying for mortgages. You may be able to get "pre-approved" for a loan so you'll know the maximum amount you can afford to pay for a home. If you're seen as a poor credit risk, you either won't qualify for a loan or will often have to accept a loan with a higher rate of interest.

Be aware, also, that your credit worthiness may be downgraded if "too many" creditors have looked at your credit record. Your credit rating is based upon many factors and one of them that can hurt you is the number of times creditors or lenders have looked at your credit report. Be careful in giving too many authorizations to creditors when shopping for car loans, home loans or other purposes.

96. How to take years off your home payments

When you buy a home, your loan (the mortgage) usually takes 30 years to be paid off. If you buy your first house at 30, you'll still be making mortgage payments until age 60.

There are two easy ways to avoid 30 years of mortgage payments. One way is to take out a 15-year loan. With a 15-year loan, the monthly payments are higher but the interest rate is lower. (The payments are higher because you are paying off the loan twice as fast.)

Another way to pay your loan off faster and save interest is to have a 30-year loan and make extra payments in an amount you determine. A small but regular extra payment can result in your saving interest payments equal to 50% or more of the original loan amount.

97. Wills and trusts

Sooner or later, either you will need to have a will and/or a trust or you will be affected by one. It doesn't hurt to start learning about them now.

A *will* is a legal document that goes into effect after a person has passed away and tells who will inherit the person's assets, who will manage the assets and who will take care of the person's minor children.

A *trust* is a similar document dealing just with assets. Some trusts are effective when the creator of the trust is alive and some come into play after a death.

Wills may need to go through the court process upon a death. Many trusts, such as a "living trust," may avoid the court process.

If a person doesn't sign a will or trust, the state writes a will for the deceased person. The state says who will inherit assets, who will raise the children and when children will get total control of their share of any inheritance. The state's will also usually produces the worst tax results and higher legal and court-related costs.

98. Simplify your life

Simplification is becoming a major trend.

One way to deal with a shortage of time and money while improving your lifestyle is to simplify it.

By reducing your material needs, you gain freedom to make

career changes and life decisions without being shackled by a financial ball and chain.

Reducing paperwork and getting financial control
Here are some first steps that can help.

1. Consider automatic payouts for mortgage payments and health insurance premiums as well as automatic deductions from your paycheck or checking account for investments, retirement and college savings.
2. Have your paychecks automatically deposited.
3. Limit and consolidate the number of investments, mutual funds and retirement plans to a manageable number so your assets are diversified, but not too many in number. Too many small investments can lead to chaos and cause you to give up on trying to monitor what's happening where.
4. Limit yourself to one credit card (two at most) and pay off the outstanding balance every month.

99. Seven real-life money-smart skills

Congratulations! After finishing this book, you should now know how to:
1. Think about and save money
2. Make a budget and pay bills on time
3. Be a savvy shopper
4. Open and balance a checking account
5. Find and use the right credit card
6. Deal with college costs
7. Begin investing

Appendix

Brain teasers

Here are some brain teasers to solve yourself or to quiz your parents on (the answers start on page 137):

1. What are the earliest coins that have been found and what was unique about them?

2. What's the earliest paper money and what was it made from?

3. Who's the father of paper money in the United States?

4. Who came up with the ideas of "cents" and "dimes"?

5. When were credit cards first used?

6. When did ATMs start appearing?

7. What's been the biggest money around?

8. Where does the word "money" come from?

9. Where does the word "salary" come from?

10. Where does the word "bank" come from?

11. Why were checks a big change in banking?

12. How far back can we trace inflation (i.e., the increased cost of living going up)?

13. Where does the word "dollar" come from?

14. If inflation (the cost of living) goes up 6% per year, how long will it take for an $8 movie to cost $16?

15. If you get 10% interest on your money, how long will it take for your money to double?

16. Assume Sally. age 20, puts $2,000 per year into a retirement plan for 3 years and then stops making any contributions. Assume Joe, age 40, puts $2,000 per year into a similar plan for 20 years. If both retirement plans grow at 10% interest per year, who will have more money at age 60?

Answers to Brain Teasers

1. It depends upon your definition of coins. Around 600 B.C., the first coins were made from electrum. Electrum is a combination of gold and silver that occurs naturally. These coins were made in Lydia (now part of Turkey). The coins were made into the same size and weight and this turned out to be a big time-saver in commerce. Until then, silver and gold had to be weighed each time a trade or transaction was made. With standard coins, all that was necessary was to count the coins to complete a trade.

A thousand years earlier, China had its own form of coins—knife money and bronze spade money. Knives and spades were considered coins because they were virtually identical, had a guaranteed value and were deemed official by the state.

2. China was the first to use paper money around the year 1000. It was made from the bark of mulberry trees. Leaves from these trees, you may recall, are fed to caterpillars to produce silk. Marco Polo later wrote about this unique form of money.

3. Ben Franklin. He's on the $100 bill.

4. Thomas Jefferson. It was his idea of using the decimal system with "cent" from the Latin word for hundred and "dime" from the Latin for tenth.

5. The 1950s.

6. The 1970s.

7. In Yap (part of Micronesia in the Pacific), they've used stone money. Some of the stone disks have been up to 13 feet across. Although stone money may not handy to use for shopping, it's sure hard to steal.

8. The Romans made a new silver coin, the denarius, in the temple of Juno Moneta. From Moneta, we have the word "money."

9. "Salary" comes from the Latin word "sal" meaning "of salt." Salt was a form of money from China to the Mediterranean. Besides its value in preserving and flavoring food, its pureness allowed it to be cut into standardized sizes to be used for purposes ranging from paying soldiers to trading for food.

10. Back in the 1300s, Italian banks were established. The word "bank" comes from the word "bench." Bankers transacted their business sitting on benches.

11. Until checks were invented by the Medici Bank in Florence, Italy, the only way to withdraw money from a bank was to appear in person and ask for a withdrawal.

12. Roman emperors needed to deal with inflation when paying their soldiers. Back in 46 B.C., soldiers received around 225 denarii under Julius Caesar's reign. Two hundred years or so later, Septimus Severus had to pay 600 denarii in 200 A.D. Twenty years later, inflation really took off and Maximinus paid 1,800 denarii.

13. Back in the early 1500s, in Bohemia (part of Germany), a

new coin known as the thaler appeared. Soon any large silver coin was called a thaler. Over time, a thaler was called a dollar in England.

14. 12 years. Use the Rule of 72. Divide 72 by 6 (the 6% inflation rate) and the result is 12. In this case, the rule tells you how long it will take for prices to double rather than the size of your investments. For more information, see Money-Smart Way #69.

15. At 10% per year interest, it will take 7.2 years for your money to double. You use the Rule of 72 again to get this answer. Divide 72 by the number (10) representing the yearly growth rate (10%) and the answer is 7.2 years. For more information, see Money-Smart Way #65.

16. Sally will. Through compound growth (letting her money work for her for a longer period of time), she'll have around $225,000 and Joe will have around $114,000. With just three contributions at an earlier age, Sally will have almost twice as much as Joe. Imagine how much she'd have if she continued to make the contributions. For more information, see Money-Smart Way #66.

Internet Sites of Interest

Note: New Internet sites are appearing all the time and the addresses of existing sites may change from time to time.

College
Cost Calculations:
http://www.collegeboard.org
http://www.finaid.org
Financial aid sources: http://www.finaid.org
Scholarships:
http://www.fastweb.com
http://www.finaid.org
http://www.scholarships.com
State savings plans: http://www.collegesavings.org
Student loan repayment:
http://www.salliemae.com
http://www.usagroup.com

Consumer information
http://www.pueblo.gsa.gov

Coupons
http://www.e-coupon.com
http://www.storecoupon.com

Credit reporting agencies
http://www.equifax.com
http://www.experian.com
http://www.tuc.com

Debt reduction and counseling
http://www.nfcc.org

Personal finance
http://www.quicken.com

Searching the Net
http://www.av.com
http://www.google.com
http://www.infind.com

Shopping on the Net
Bots (robots)
http://www.bottomdollar.com
http://www.buycentral.com
http://www.dealtime.com
http://www.mysimon.com
http://www.pricescan.com
Merchant rating service
http://www.bizrate.com
Money-saving ideas
http://www.savvystudent.com
http://www.stretcher.com
http://www.thefrugal shopper.com

Social Security
http://www.ssa.gov

Volunteering
http://www.SERVEnet.org
http://www.ysa.org

Books of Interest

If you're an entrepreneur or want to be one, take a look at *FAIL-PROOF YOUR BUSINESS: Beat the Odds and Be Successful* by Paul E. Adams. While there are many books on entrepreneurship, there is none on how to avoid failing. This book shows the telltale warning signs of failure and how to deal with them. It also shows how to prevent potentially fatal business problems from occurring in the first place as well as how to save a business that's already in trouble. In addition, this book offers special, often overlooked strategies for business success.

THE GENERATION X MONEY BOOK: Achieving Security and Independence by Don Silver is a step-by-step, easy-to-read guide that offers evolutionary money management solutions for Gen Xers. These 40 million individuals born between 1965 and 1976 will encounter dramatically new definitions of jobs, money and career, not to mention retirement plans.

BABY BOOMER RETIREMENT: 65 Simple Ways to Protect Your Future by Don Silver is a one-stop resource for busy boomers who want to take control and protect their children, their parents and their financial future.

Adams-Hall Publishing
1/800-888-4452
www.adams-hall.com

Index

Index

G

Gifts
  for college education, 67, 69-70
Giving to others, 49-51
Goals
  financial, 12, 113-14
  setting, 12, 113-14

H

Health insurance, 127
Hope Credits, 71
Home. *See* Real estate

I

Identity theft
  preventing, 47
Impulsive shopping, 28
Income tax. *See also* Capital gains
  tax, Tax deferral and Tax-free
  income
  capital gains and, 111-12
  credit card interest and, 42
  deducting interest and, 131
  IRA and, 108-111
  mutual funds and, 106-07
  ordinary, 111-12
  Roth IRA, 95-96, 108-110, 112
  stocks and, 111
  traditional IRA and, 108-110
Individual retirement account. *See*
  IRA
Inflation
  college education and, 65

effects of, 99-101, 108
Rule of 72 and, 100-01
Insurance. *See* Disability insurance,
  Health insurance, Life insurance
Interest
  credit cards and, 41-42
  401(k) loans and, 121-22
  mortgage and, 131
Internet. See Web sites.
  shopping on, 35-36, 141
Investments
  right, 112-113
  saving through, 91-114
IRA. *See also* Retirement plans
  beneficiary designations and, 130
  conduit, 122
  conversion to Roth, 109
  distributions from, 109-110
  Education, 70
  rollovers to, 122
  Roth, 95-96, 108-110
  traditional, 108-110
  withdrawals and, 109-110

J

Jobs. *See* Work
Junior colleges, 63-64, 68

L

Life insurance
  beneficiary designations and, 130
  cash value, 129-30
  need for, 128
  soundness of companies and, 130